# GROWING BY GRACE

## Sanctification and Counseling

## by Jay E. Adams

"But grow by the grace and the knowledge
of our Lord and Savior Jesus Christ."
II Peter 3:18

TIMELESS TEXTS
Stanley, NC

# Contents

# Introduction

At the outset, I want to explain why I have placed *sanctification* and *counseling* in juxtaposition in this book. To some (particularly those who believe in eclectic counseling) it may seem odd – indeed, even foolish – to do so. To those who believe in biblical counseling, however, the explanation that I shall give will doubtless make sense.

I chose to consider the relationship of sanctification to counseling in order to determine the implications for counseling that may arise. It is biblical counseling, then, that is the concern of the book; the scriptural teaching about sanctification is of concern only as it throws light upon the practice of nouthetic[1] counseling.

My emphasis upon counseling, however, must in no way be understood as downplaying the care that has been taken in discussing the biblical truths concerning sanctification. Without adequate attention given to the exposition of this pivotal doctrine, its implications for counseling would be flawed. It is, therefore, possible to study the doctrine of sanctification itself as I have set it forth here as well as to study how this teaching impinges upon biblical counseling. All doctrine has important implications for counseling, but I think you will see why I have called sanctification *pivotal* to pastoral counseling.

"Okay, what you have done is clear. But why do it? What is the great significance that sanctification has for counseling?"

---

1. For those not familiar with the term, the word "nouthetic" is a transliteration of a word in the Greek New Testament, which is found particularly in the writings of the Apostle Paul. The Greek word, *nouthesia*, was brought over into English because it is larger than the English term "counsel" and because it is free from many of the unwanted associations that the word "counsel" carries. *Nouthesia* contains three elements; it speaks of *change* that is brought about by verbal *confrontation* out of *concern* for the one who is counseled. In this book, for the sake of convenience, unless otherwise indicated, the word "counsel" is used interchangeably with the word *nouthesia*. For more detail, consult my book *Competent to Counsel*.

This question is legitimate. Of course, since this book is concerned precisely with setting forth the implications of the doctrine for counseling, in one sense, the entire book is my answer to that question. Allow me to summarize in the introduction why I have written this book.

Because counseling is so intimately connected to sanctification, if one's understanding of sanctification is faulty, that will negatively affect his counseling. Because counseling is an aspect of sanctification, or because in so many situations it is so important to proper Christian growth, sanctification often depends upon effective, biblical counseling. In short, the two are so closely bound together that counseling cannot be properly carried on apart from a correct understanding of sanctification. And in those cases where biblical counseling is required, sanctification will not take place as it should unless the correct relationship and implications of each are understood and properly worked out. In other words, each depends upon the other. Given that fact, I think you will agree that it is altogether appropriate to study the symbiotic relationship between counseling and sanctification.

## Chapter One
# Why There is a Need for Sanctification

Through one representative act of rebellion, Adam plunged the entire human race into sin. By eating the forbidden fruit, he caused two things to happen: from birth all men (Jesus excepted) became guilty and all men became corrupt. God deals with *guilt* by the *act* of *justifying* those who believe the gospel, and He deals with *corruption* by the *process* of *sanctifying* them. Sanctification is needed, therefore, because of man's corruption.

What does it mean that all are born corrupt (or polluted)? Essentially, it means that human nature has been so warped by sin that, apart from the grace of God freely granted to those God determines to save, men cannot do anything that pleases God.[1] As Paul put it in Romans 8:8: "Those who are in the flesh can't please God." Why is that?

The reason for this inability[2] is that the whole person, inner and outer, has become oriented away from God and His will, and his nature is now oriented toward sin. As Isaiah put it, both man's "ways" (outer words and actions) and "thoughts" (inner understanding, desires, and intents) are, in this manner, so distorted as to need radical change: "For My thoughts are not your thoughts, neither are your ways My ways" (Isaiah 55:8). That is why God says, "Let the wicked forsake his way, and the unrighteous man his thoughts; and let him return to the LORD, and He will have compassion on him, and to our God, for He will abundantly pardon" (Isaiah 55:7). Clearly, God is displeased with both our ways and our thoughts – so much so that He calls for *repentance*: "forsake" and "return" are the two operative verbs in Isaiah 55, verse 7 quoted above.

The concept of repentance in the Old and the New Tes-

---

1. In Adam the intellectual and moral aspects of the "image of God" with which man was endowed by creation (Genesis 1:27) were lost and must be "renewed" (cf. Colossians 3:10; Ephesians 4:24).

2. In Greek, *ou dunetai. Ou* is a strong negative.

taments includes both the inner and the outer elements. The Hebrew term *shuv* means both to "return" and "turn," referring to outer change that repentance effects; the Greek word *metanoieo* means "to rethink so as to change one's mind," and refers to inner change that brings about the turning. In other words, the former emphasizes the need for a change of ways, while the latter focuses upon the change in thinking that leads to the change of ways.

There are those who claim to have truly repented because either their *thinking* or their *behavior* (but not both) more or less conforms to God's Word, yet in God's sight, neither conforms. To understand or think differently, without a subsequent change in one's *ways* (behavior or way of life) means that the understanding and the thinking are superficial and ingenuine. On the other hand, to "change one's ways," without a change of heart which affects one's thoughts and intents, is pharisaical and equally unacceptable. In Isaiah 55, God makes it clear that the problem is twofold; it is an internal-outward problem. Thus, there must be a decided change in *both* areas of one's life. Since the whole person sins, the whole person must be changed. In another chapter, we shall see how that two-fold change takes place. But for now, let us consider further this need for sanctification as it pertains to fallen men and women.

Corruption of man's nature, as we have seen, makes him unable to please God in both his *thoughts* and his *ways*. Those two highly descriptive words are Isaiah's shorthand for all of human life. To speak of a person's thoughts and ways as unacceptable in God's eyes is to speak of him as *totally* unable to please Him.[1] Paul agrees with Isaiah. There is not one scintilla of holiness (or a desire for it) in human nature as it comes forth at birth. Nothing about it is ori-

---

1. Total depravity means that every aspect of a person has been corrupted by the fall; it does not mean that he is as sinful as he might possibly become. It does mean, however, that there is *nothing* in a person's unregenerate nature which can or will respond favorably to the things of God (see I Corinthians 2:14). This fact is of extreme importance

ented toward God or pleases Him. Rather, human beings are born corrupt persons who, because of this corruption, develop thoughts and ways that result in living "in the flesh." In Romans 8:4 and 5, Paul mentions walking according to the flesh and setting the mind on fleshly things. These words correspond to Isaiah's "ways" and "thoughts."

By "flesh" Paul refers to the lifestyle that is produced by the sinful nature. *If* an unbeliever were to desire or attempt to love and serve God (which he *would* not do), he *could* not do it. Why? Because his nature and his lifestyle (which, as we have seen, includes one's thoughts and ways) prohibit him from doing so. As a result, for a human being to please God he must have both a change of nature and a change of lifestyle.

The Holy Spirit alone can rectify this disastrous two-fold problem. He alone can change man's nature, and it is the Spirit, dwelling within the believer, Who fights successfully against the flesh throughout his life, thus enabling him to become more and more like Jesus Christ. The simple fact is that because the unbeliever does not possess the Spirit of Christ, he does not belong to Christ and cannot be considered one of God's sons. "If anybody doesn't have Christ's Spirit, he isn't His" (Romans 8:9; see also v. 14). These grave deficiencies (apart from a work of the Spirit in him subsequent to birth) make it impossible for him even to repent and believe the gospel. The work of the Spirit that enables him to do so is called the "new birth." When a person is born again,[1] the process of sanctification begins to

---

to biblical counselors, who should not knowingly counsel unbelievers. If unbelieving counselees do not please God by their present lifestyles (Romans 8:8), there is no biblical reason to help them develop different lifestyles that would be every bit as displeasing to Him. Indeed, it would be sin for the counselor to do so. Truly biblical counselors seek to *evangelize* unbelievers, not to *counsel* them.

1. Or, as the word *anothen* possibly means, born "from above" (John 3:3, 7). But see John 3:4 where Nicodemus' words "a second time"

take place. It is then and then alone that counseling may profitably be carried on.[1] So it is evident that sanctification occurs only in those who have had a change of nature and repented.

All of this is important for the counselor to know. Sanctification, as we shall see, involves both inner and outer growth toward holiness that is produced by the grace of God through His Holy Spirit.[2] Since the problem involves thoughts and ways that displease God, the remedy, as in repentance, must also reach to both aspects of the one who is being sanctified. The fruit of the Spirit, which of course means the products of His work in the believer, reveal qualities that are both inner and outer: "...the Spirit's fruit is love, joy, peace, patience, kindness, goodness, faithfulness, meekness, self-control" (Galatians 5:22, 23). Clearly, those qualities involve both inner and outer transformations in the person who, born only the first time, possesses none of them.[3]

Note also that it is not merely the change of one's orientation that brings about the new sanctified lifestyle.

---

seem to parallel *anothen*, indicating that "again" is the preferred translation of this word that, apart from context, may be translated either way.

1. We shall consider what necessitates counseling at a later point in the book.

2. In Romans 1:4, the Holy Spirit is called "the Spirit of holiness" because it is His work to produce holiness. Sanctification comes only through Him.

3. The world speaks of these things as though men may possess them apart from the work of the Spirit, but what the world describes by the misuse of these labels are qualities that are actually quite different from the fruit of the Spirit. His fruit is always positively related to God on a vertical level; the former (in contrast) are humanistically related to man on a purely horizontal one. This distinction points to the quite different characters that Christians develop from those that are found in non-Christians. Moreover, their worldviews – which affect all they do and think – are quite distinct. And because the love, joy, peace, and so on, that pagan counseling systems claim to bring about are ersatz, the biblical counselor will not be duped into believing that the methods proposed in these systems will produce that which, according the Scriptures is due solely to sanctification by the Spirit.

Changed thinking and living depend not only upon the working of the Spirit as He applies His Word,[1] but also upon Him as He cooperates with the believer, motivating and enabling him to work out the possibilities of the new nature and the new lifestyle that is developing.[2] You can see, then, that the process which we call sanctification is not simple but complex. The counselor must not only understand the process, but also must know how to work with counselees in such a manner that he does not overlook any aspect of it, or overemphasize one to the detriment of the rest. There is always the temptation to do so. Knowledge of the ins and outs of sanctification will go a long way toward helping him to resist the temptation. Change is not brought about by the counselor or by the counselee alone; change is a divine/human activity. All of these factors, as you can see, make it vital for the biblical counselor to understand and, as he counsels, to continually remember all the elements of the process.

So then, while the need for sanctification is great, the need to understand and appreciate it fully is equally important. Without this process at work in the life of the believer, his lifestyle following the new birth would not be unlike that which he lived before it. So since we agree on that – don't we? – let's proceed with our study.

---

1. See also John 17:17, "Sanctify them by the truth; Your Word is truth!"

2. See also Philippians 2:13: "...it is God Who is producing in you both the willingness and the ability to do the things that please Him."

## Chapter Two
# What is Sanctification Anyway?

We have seen already that sanctification is needed to deal with the scourge of corruption inherited from our first father, Adam.[1] We have learned that sanctification is not the same as justification: justification is an instantaneous act that deals with the guilt of our sin, while sanctification is an ongoing process that deals with the corruption that leads us into more and more sin. Like repentance, which has to do with both inner and outer factors, so too sanctification is a two-fold process that relates to both the inner and the outer lifestyle – how one thinks and how he acts. So far, so good. But what, precisely, is sanctification?

Let's begin by taking a look at the biblical terms associated with sanctification, which themselves tell us a lot about the process. The Greek words *hagiasmos* (sanctification, holiness), *hagiazo* (to sanctify) and *hagios* (holy) are terms that all refer to that which is "separated." The separation envisioned is both *from* sin and Satan and *to* God and righteousness.

In writing to the church, the Apostle Peter said, "...[you] are chosen according to the foreknowledge of God the Father, that *by the Spirit's sanctification*[2] you may obey..." (I Peter 1:2; emphasis mine). Paul wrote, "Now this is God's will: your sanctification" (I Thessalonians 4:3), and "God didn't call us to uncleanness, but rather to sanctification" (I Thessalonians 4:7). Thus in Romans 6:19[b] he explained,

In the same way that you presented your members as slaves to uncleanness and lawlessness to bring

---

1. In addition to which, as a result of that corruption, we have contributed to the human legacy of sin by means of our own attitudes and acts. But each develops his own individual style of sinning. So, not only must the corruption of our nature, but also the lifestyles that each has developed as the outworking of that corruption, be overcome.

2. See also Romans 15:16: "in order that the offering up of the Gentiles may be acceptable, being sanctified by the Holy Spirit."

about more lawlessness, now you must present your
members as slaves of righteousness to bring about
sanctification.

And, as a final sample of New Testament usage, consider
Paul's benediction:

May the God of peace Himself sanctify you completely; may your entire being – spirit and soul and
body – be kept blameless for the coming of our Lord
Jesus Christ (I Thessalonians 5:23).

Obviously, as you can see from these few New Testament
citations, sanctification is an important matter that extends
to the whole of life. The Christian is, as Paul said, "called to
sanctification." Becoming sanctified is a lifelong task
assigned to every believer by virtue of becoming a believer.
Sanctification, then, is an integral part of the Christian life.

The Old Testament term *qadosh* (sanctified, holy) and
those derivatives from it, bear essentially the same meaning as the New Testament words, though because of temple
ritual and Mosaic law there is a vast application of sanctification to things, places, events, times, and so forth, that is
not found in the New Testament. The word refers to persons whose lives are consecrated (separated) to God, or of
things (such as the pots and pans used in the temple) set
apart for sacred uses. In Numbers 7:1, we read that Moses
"...finished setting up the tabernacle and had anointed and
sanctified it with all its equipment, including the altar and
its utensils which he likewise anointed and sanctified..."[1]
(Berkeley). In all such instances, the sanctification, or setting aside, is a one-time thing (though the effects were last-
ing), whereas the personal sanctification with which we are
principally concerned in this book is a growth process.

Prophetically speaking of Jesus' resurrection, David
wrote, "You will not leave My soul in sheol, nor will you

---

1. These items, thus, were *set aside* for special use, and that use
alone.

allow Your Holy One to see corruption" (Psalm 16:10, NKJV). God, and His Son, of course, were always set apart as the only true God and therefore quite distinct (holy, i.e., separate) from all other (false) gods. There is nothing progressive about Their set-apart-ness.

That which was "holy" in the Mosaic law was distinguished from that which was "common" or "unclean" (cf. Leviticus 10:10). Although sanctification in the Old Testament most often referred to ritual or ceremonial holiness rather than holiness of lifestyle, the intent of this set-apart, godly relationship of things and people was to symbolize the spiritual relationship that is more clearly spelled out in the New Testament. The clean/unclean system of the Old Testament was intended to teach that all of life (what you eat, what you wear, etc.) is to be consecrated (set apart) to God. That teaching is one that counselors today must continue to inculcate in counselees.

As the Old Testament priest was holy (Leviticus 21:6), so now that all believers are declared to be priests, they too are considered holy (I Peter 2:5, N.B. the designation a "*holy* priesthood"). In fact, every Christian, by virtue of his justification before God, is considered a "saint" (cf. Philippians 1:1), or "holy one." That is to say, by a once-for-all act of God, he has been *set apart* from others to love and serve God. Thus, the New Testament does not entirely abandon the idea of groups or individuals being set apart once-for-all by one definitive act of sanctification.[1] It is important, then, to distinguish those verses that speak of sanctification in the definitive Old Testament sense from those that speak of progressive sanctification in the New Testament sense.

---

1. See also Hebrews 10:14: "By a single offering He has perfected for all time those who are being set apart." In this verse the once-for-all "perfecting" (the granting of a perfect or completed status before God) that occurs at the time of justification is contrasted with the on-going process of "being set apart" (as one grows by grace in this life). In the verse, the verb used is *teleioo* (note the contrast with verse 1 where it also occurs).

Often the progressive sense of sanctification is spoken of in terms of "growing," "learning," and the like (II Peter 3:18; Titus 3:14) rather than by the use of words such as "sanctified."

This definitive, instantaneous Old Testament "setting apart" in name and status is but a precursor of what God expects the believer to *become*.[1] Unlike the Old Testament pot or pan that was set apart for temple use, the New Testament "saint," designated as such at conversion, must become saintly[2] (something that the lifeless, inert thing could not do). In other words, the "saint" is one who has been "set apart" (positionally) for the purpose of becoming "set apart" (in his actual lifestyle). He is to live up to his status more and more.

Sanctification, then, is a significant matter. No counselor can safely fail to understand that his counseling is intended to assist counselees in this process of becoming more thoroughly set apart (sanctified). Anything that does not contribute to growth from sinful thought and behavior to righteous thinking and ways of living has no part in counseling.

It is wise for counselors to learn about the definitive and the progressive aspects of sanctification so as to be able to call upon counselees to approximate in daily living what they are reckoned to be before God. In Romans 6:11, Paul wrote, "So too you must count [or reckon] yourselves to be dead to sin, but living for God in Christ Jesus." Again, in this verse, the two aspects of salvation – that which is reckoned (counted; one's status before God) and that which we are in the process of becoming – appear in relation to one another. "You are dead," Paul is saying, "so live in that light.

---

1. The word "marriage" may refer to the legal ceremony in which one becomes "man and wife," or to all that follows. Similarly, the word "sanctification" may refer to the legal relationship (status) established by God at justification or to all that follows.

2. That is, more and more set apart from sin and to righteousness in his thinking and ways (see the discussion of Isaiah 55:8 in chapter 1).

Sin has been put aside once-for-all in Christ (though not in your daily 'living'). That means that daily you are obligated to live up to your status. So I am exhorting you to live more and more for God instead of for sin."

"How should one live?" a counselee may ask. The astute counselor answers, "According to your status as a saint," or words to that effect. Indeed, because of the *what-you-are/ what-you-must-become* dynamic found everywhere in the New Testament, you may go on to tell your counselee, "You see, by telling you how He regards you – what you have become in Christ – and because God has spelled this out not only by the teachings of the Bible but also by the example of His Son, He has made it clear that by His grace you are capable of growing into the 'stature' of Jesus Christ" (Ephesians 4:13).

Look at the sixth chapter of Romans a bit more carefully. Here, Paul's concern is to show the inconsistency of "continuing in sin." It is inconsistent for the Christian to do so, he argues, because grace has transformed both the believer's status (standing) before God and his ability to live righteously. All of this he has been explaining in the previous chapter. In chapter 5:20, Paul points out that grace is more than a match for sin: "Where sin abounded, grace far more abounded." So, he asks in chapter 6:1, "Should we continue in sin so that grace might abound?" The thought runs this way: someone might think, "if grace covers all sin, then why not sin all the more so that there will be an even greater abundance of grace to cover it?" But that is absurd, he responds (v. 2). After all, in God's reckoning, "you have died to sin" – that is your status before Him. How then can you even *think* of living in sin? Then comes his clinching argument.

The argument that backs up his statement in verse 2 is this: Don't you know that you were baptized into Christ and what the implications of that fact are?[1] Presumably, some

---

1. Many counselees don't know this because they were never

would say, "I guess I don't." Well, let me tell you about it, is Paul's retort. By being baptized into Christ, you were baptized into His death. Note that the verse doesn't speak of being baptized into water, but of being baptized into *Christ*. That distinction is important.

But what does it mean to be baptized into Christ? Paul goes on to explain. By being baptized into Christ, you were baptized into Christ's *death*, which is what I have been talking about – because you *died* by virtue of being "in Christ," you are considered to have *died* to sin. By this baptism into Christ, Paul goes on to explain, you were baptized into His death, His burial, and His resurrection (v. 4). And just as being baptized into Christ means that you were baptized into His death, so too being baptized into Him means being baptized into His resurrection. And that means that God reckons you to have been raised to a new lifestyle ("newness of life"). So your baptism into Christ implies death to the old lifestyle and life to the new one.

Now, the importance of the phrase "baptized into Christ" is that God "counts" (or "reckons") you to have experienced all of these things that *He* experienced. Paul's favorite phrase, "in Christ," used throughout his letters, corresponds to the concept he sets forth here: those who are "in Christ" are considered such by virtue of being "baptized" *into* Him. The word "baptize" (*baptizo*) has been wrongly interpreted to mean "to dip" (that is, to put into and *remove*); there is another word (*bapto*) that carries the meaning "to dip."[1] The word *baptizo* ("baptize"), on the other hand, means "to put together, to unite." The idea behind *baptizo* in this text then, is to place things together *so as to stay together*. That understanding is plainly in view in this passage in Romans where the believer is thought of as *united* and *identified with* Christ. There is no idea of dip-

---

taught it. So it is wise for a counselor to learn Paul's argument and, from time to time, to use it to encourage righteous living.

1. *Bapto*, "to dip," is found in Luke 16:24.

ping him into Christ and removing him once again.[1] Precisely the opposite! The idea of such a union with Christ is that he remains in Him: all that He has done is attributed to the believer as if he had experienced it himself.

So Paul says, in effect, "If you have the whole (baptism into Christ) – *all* that Christ experienced – you have the part of that whole that corresponds to what I am teaching." By virtue of being baptized into Christ, the Christian is reckoned to have been circumcised with Christ (Colossians 2:11, 12), crucified with Christ (Galatians 2:20), to have died, been buried, and been raised with Christ (Romans 6:4) and to be seated with Him in heavenly places at the right hand of the Father (Colossians 3:1; Ephesians 2:6). The whole of Christ's work is attributed to the believer because he is identified with (baptized into) Him.

Because this vital biblical concept is foreign even to many counselors, let me take the time to make it as clear as I can by means of an illustration. If I place a bean "into" a jar, the bean is "in" the jar and, as a result, identified with it. Wherever the jar goes, the bean also goes because it was introduced *into* the jar and now is *in* the jar. Put the jar on a table, the bean is on the table. Place the jar on the floor, the bean is on the floor. Raise it up to a shelf and the bean is raised up as well – all because the bean is *in the jar.* Just so, the Christian is viewed as going through all that Christ did by virtue of being united with Him (cf. Romans 6:5[2])

---

1. See also I Corinthians 12:13 where the believer is said to have been baptized (*baptizo*) by the Spirit into the body of Christ (the invisible church). Certainly, one isn't dipped into the body of Christ and then removed! Rather, by the Spirit he is "united" or "joined" with God's church. This concept of being "united, joined, and identified with" is the essence of baptism (cf. I Corinthians 10:2, where the Israelites were baptized "into Moses"). Baptism with water is the uniting ordinance; one joins the visible church by water baptism as he joins the invisible church by Spirit baptism.

2. "If we have become *united with Him* in a death like His..." (emphasis mine). Here Paul explains in unmistakable terms that being baptized into Christ is being "united with Him."

13

by Spirit[1] baptism.

Paul emphasizes death, burial, and resurrection not because baptism into Christ means *only* that, but rather, because it pictures entrance into the *whole* of Christ's experiences, including baptism into His death and resurrection, which is the point that he is making in the passage. He is saying that, if you are counted to have died, been buried, and risen with Christ to newness of life, then live like it! Live the new life that you have in Him; let your everyday life more closely approximate your status before God.

So in this passage, and in many more like it, you see that the essence of sanctification is simply this: becoming what you are. That is to say, becoming in daily life what you are already reckoned to be by virtue of being in Christ.[2] This process is a daily one, as we shall see later on; but it is the dynamic by which every nouthetic counselor encourages the believer to grow out of his sinful thoughts and ways into God's righteous thoughts and ways. Sanctification thus provides the pattern for discipleship, change during counseling, and daily growth.

---

1. Plainly, there is not a drop of water in Romans 6. To introduce the idea of water baptism into the passage is to intrude it rather than find it there. Water baptism certainly does not produce the results of which Paul speaks, but Spirit baptism does.

2. The whole put on/put off dynamic found in Ephesians 4 and Colossians 3 (and detailed in my book *The Christian Counselor's Manual*) is a further example of this approach to sanctification. Paul says in effect that in Christ you are a new person; so now, in everyday life, put off the old person that you were, along with his sinful ways, and put on the new person that you have become in Christ with His new, holy ways.

## Chapter Three
# What Makes Sanctification Possible?

Obviously, since people are by birth unable to please God,[1] and therefore are not proper subjects for counseling, something must intervene before an individual may be accepted for counseling. What is it? Plainly, he must become a Christian.

But to speak of one becoming a Christian is not like saying that he has become a member of a political party or even a partner in a business. Becoming a disciple of Jesus Christ is a decision that is made not wholly by the person himself. Given his inability and his adverse orientation, what enables him to turn in the opposite direction, repent, and believe the gospel? In asking that, we are probing the more ultimate question – "Why is it that one person becomes a Christian and another does not?"

Jesus answered that question when He spoke about the Father "drawing" people to Him (John 6:44). And He enlarged the point in speaking about His death on the cross when He said that by being "lifted up" He would "draw all sorts of people"[2] to Himself (John 12:32). In other words,

---

1. See also Psalm 51:5; 58:3; Ephesians 2:3. This last reference, in which Paul says that "by nature we too were children of wrath," is interesting. In Greek usage, and elsewhere in the New Testament (I Corinthians 11:14), *phusis* (nature) does not always mean "determined by genetic code," but rather, "things as they are without anything being done to make them so." It is the person or thing as it (he) is in itself (himself). One does not have to *do* anything to *make* himself a child of wrath. Indeed, unless something is done to him, he simply (or by nature) is such.

2. The verb, *elko,* means "to draw, drag, and pull," and clearly refers to the exertion of an outside force (not necessarily hostile or resisted). The phrase "all sorts of people," as I have translated it in the CCNT, is more accurate than the KJV which has "all men." Elsewhere, John put it this way in the book of Revelation when he spoke of the redeemed being "from every nation and tribe and people and tongue" (Revelation 7:9). For more on this important matter, see my book *Christian Living in the World.*

His sacrificial, penal, substitutionary death would be the occasion for the drawing. These verses unmistakably teach that in order to transform one's wholly corrupt nature there must be the imposition of an outside Force. That drawing power is the effectual force of the Holy Spirit.

In the Bible there are various way of picturing this transforming imposition. We have already noted Jesus' words to Nicodemus, "You must be born again." Consider this passage for a minute. John the Baptist came calling people to repentance. As a sign of repentance, he baptized with water those who repented. Jesus, however, came baptizing with the Spirit (In John 1:33, the Baptist himself sets forth the contrast). Nicodemus came as a representative of[1] the Pharisees (John 3:1). The Pharisees refused to repent and be baptized by John (Luke 7:30; John 3:11, 12). Thus, when Jesus spoke of being baptized with water and with the Spirit (John 3:5), He meant that they must repent[2] and believe in Him.

Jesus spoke to Nicodemus both as a representative and as an individual. Note the important interplay of singulars and plurals. In addition to speaking to Nicodemus as an individual, Jesus said, "you *all* [all of you Pharisees] must be born again" (v. 7). And He also spoke not only of Himself alone (using "I"), but also of John and Himself together (note the use of "we" and "our" as well in v. 11). The Pharisees had refused to believe in John or in Jesus, who jointly came proclaiming God's message. Evidence of unbelief in John's message was their refusal to be baptized by him. Rather than follow the example of his fellow Pharisees, who rejected what John and he said, Jesus urged Nicodemus to believe and receive both baptisms (John 3:5).

---

1. The word "of" probably ought to have the force of an ablative and be translated "from."

2. The "water" in John 3:5 stands for the *meaning* and *purpose* of John's baptism: repentance (Mark 1:4). Jesus did not mean that water baptism brought about any inner change; it was a sign that it had already taken place.

Now this new birth into a new kind of life is produced, as Jesus explained, by the Holy Spirit: "what is born of the Spirit is spirit" (John 3:6). That is to say, spiritual life is produced by His action in the inner person. The Spirit is the outer Force Who brings about the inner change. As Paul said, "God's love has been poured into our hearts through the Holy Spirit Who was given to us" (Romans 5:5). This statement and the words of Jesus to Nicodemus appear to be references to the prophecy of Ezekiel who wrote,

> I will sprinkle clean water upon you, and you will be cleansed from all your impurities.... A new heart, too, I will give you, and a new spirit I will put within you. I will take the heart of stone out of your flesh, and I will give you a heart of flesh. I will put My Spirit within you and cause you to walk in My statutes, and you shall observe My ordinances and do them (Ezekiel 36:25–27, Berkeley).

As the Agent of the Father, the Spirit does what a person cannot do for himself: He transforms unregenerate persons into regenerate ones. He changes the "heart" so that the whole person is now oriented toward God and toward doing His commandments (v. 27). The "new spirit," that which is "born of the Spirit" (John 3:6) is an attitude of acceptance and desire to do what God wills. The old heart was stony. That means that it was impervious and resistant to the things of God. It was cold, hard, and lifeless. Now the newly implanted heart that replaces the one that the Spirit removed is warm, alive to spiritual things, and open to the teachings of God's Word.

A slightly different way of expressing these ideas is found in Ephesians 2:1, 4, and 5, where Paul pictures the transformation in terms of the resurrection of those who were "dead in trespasses and sins." He speaks of those who were spiritually dead being "made alive" (v. 5). The outside Force that raises the spiritually dead, according to Ephesians 2:4, once more is identified as God, the Spirit, Who, in doing so, is motivated by love. Throughout the

17

New Testament, the very close concepts of new life and resurrection from the death of sin to live for Christ are used to portray this change of disposition toward, and a new ability to do, God's will.

Akin to the images of being born again and being spiritually raised to newness of life is that of becoming a new creature (or creation) in Christ. Paul wrote, "Accordingly, if anybody is in Christ, he is a new creation; everything old has passed away; see, new things have come into being" (II Corinthians 5:17).[1] The problem of corruption could only be dealt with in a radical way, as these three expressions show. Apart from a new birth, resurrection, or a new creation – expressions bold enough to express the radical nature of regeneration – the individual would retain all of his old ways.

Paul is speaking of the new status, the new orientation, and the new abilities that the regenerated person has been given by the Spirit. Note as well, further along in the fifth chapter of II Corinthians, Paul adds, "For our sake He made Him Who didn't know sin to be sin, so that we might become God's righteousness by Him" (v. 21). God looked on His Son as a sin-offering, bearing our sin, so that He may look on us as possessing all His righteousness! That is the new status we have in justification. It is remarkable! Too much to express! But everywhere you turn in the New Testament, you discover that God has taken pains to show the radical change that regeneration makes. And everywhere the new, perfect righteousness – the new status – is held up as an incentive to live in accordance with it. A concise statement of this is found in Ephesians 4:1: "I urge you to walk in a way that is appropriate to the calling to which you were called."

So what do we call this transformation of our natures?

---

1. The "new creation" that the Christian becomes in Christ foreshadows the new creation of Revelation 21 and 22. There, too, old things have passed away, and all things are new (see especially Revelation 21:1, 4, 5).

Traditionally, theologians have called it "regeneration" (being made alive by a new birth), thus carrying on the concept of birth that leads to a new life. Some of us prefer to call it "quickening" (or the granting of spiritual life to a spiritually dead person). But whatever biblical figure of speech one uses, God is speaking of a change leading to the desire and the ability to please Him – something that is made possible by His transforming power (cf. Philippians 2:13). It is only because of this wholly gracious act of transformation that the regenerate person is able to glorify God and enjoy Him forever.[1]

For what, then, should the counselor who understands these things strive? First, he will never seek to counsel those he has insufficient reason to believe have been regenerated. But how can he know one way or the other? We must face the fact that he cannot know absolutely. God has not granted us the ability to look into one another's heart. In I Samuel 16:8 we read, "Man looks at the outward appearance, but the LORD looks at the heart." We do not know for sure whether or not anyone who seeks counsel has a heart of stone or flesh. God has granted us the ability to judge only his words and works. Therefore, we judge on the basis of what has been called "a credible profession of faith." That is, a profession of faith in which, after careful examination of his life and his testimony, the elders of a Bible-believing church have been satisfied sufficiently to receive him into communicant membership in their congregation. Even then, of course, there may be misjudg-

---

1. In the Old Testament, the word for "glory" (*kabod*) means "weight"; in the New Testament the word for glory (*doxa*) means "fame" or "reputation." The two were brought together by the Apostle Paul in II Corinthians 4:17 where he wrote of the "weight of glory [*doxa*]." Thus the idea of glorifying God is to so give Him the proper recognition (or weight) in all things so that His fame (or good reputation) is spread widely among all men. The task of all Christians, and the task of those who help them, is possible to achieve only by people who have been regenerated.

ments.[1] Like a Pharisee, people may pretend, and their pretense may deceive for a time. Credible membership in the church, however, is the fundamental requirement for counseling.[2]

Second, if there is sufficient doubt about a would-be counselee's regeneration, then (because of the external evidence) the counselor should refuse to counsel. He should say something like the following: "I am glad that you came for help. After listening to some of your problems, I am happy to tell you that God has solutions to every one of them. There is, however, one difficulty. The solutions of which I speak are available only to God's children. Not everyone is a child of God. If you have never become His child, then you must do so before I can counsel you. In John 1:11 and 12, He says, 'He [Jesus Christ] came to His own creation, and His own people didn't receive Him. But to as many as did receive Him He gave the right to become God's children; to those who believe in His Name.' You see, God says one must 'become' His child by 'believing.' Let me explain...." And so the counselor, for the time being, steps out of his counseling role and into the role of an evangelist, only to resume the former role if and when the "counselee" professes faith in Christ and unites with the church.

It is fruitless to attempt to counsel unregenerate persons. They cannot and will not receive the things of God and His Word (I Corinthians 2:14). And it is harmful to attempt to do so. The unregenerate "counselee" may do as you direct him, but it will not last because what he does will be done outwardly, and there will be no inward reality to sustain it. Then when it all comes apart, the person "counseled" will think that God's way (as he interprets it)

---

1. The Personal Data Inventory, a sample of which may be found in *The Christian Counselor's Manual*, has a section that is designed to help you evaluate whether or not one is a Christian. Copies of the PDI may be duplicated for use without asking for permission.

2. Apart from conclusive testimony, a counselor does not independently judge the member of such a church unregenerate.

failed! Jesus spoke of the Pharisees who, like a cup washed only on the outside, nevertheless were dirty within. We don't need new Pharisees in the church! There are plenty of them already without creating them in "counseling" sessions.

So it is important, so far as one is able to discern, to counsel only regenerate persons. If over and over again in counseling, a person who is a member of a fine church such as I have described above fails to do as God requires in His Word because he is unable to understand or do it, there may be reason to question his regeneration. In such cases, the matter, if not remedied in counseling itself, ought to be brought before the elders of his church.

So regeneration, the power of God to transform corrupt natures so as to enable individuals to begin replacing old thoughts and old ways with their biblical alternatives, is absolutely essential to proper counseling. Unlike so many well-meaning but foolish counselors who will counsel anyone, I urge you to take care about this matter and, in the end, settle for nothing less than dealing with regenerate persons.

One other implication that I wish to draw from the biblical doctrine of regeneration or quickening is that because the change is brought about by the Spirit of God – and not by the person regenerated – there is every reason to have hope in counseling. The Spirit does not begin a work that He fails to complete: "He Who began a good work among you will keep on perfecting it until the Day of Christ Jesus" (Philippians 1:6). The Spirit dwells within the believer for the very purpose of perfecting his work, with a view to presenting the believer complete in Christ. I shall have more to say about this as we continue.

## Chapter Four
# How is Sanctification Effected?

We have seen that man is wholly passive in the act of regeneration; he contributes nothing to it. God alone effects it by His Spirit. One who is *"dead* in trespasses and sins" cannot give life to himself. He cannot raise himself from the dead. He cannot *create* himself anew. He cannot *give birth* to himself. All such things,[1] if and when they occur, must be brought about by an external Force. The scriptural figures of speech – birth, resurrection, creation – powerfully speak to this fact. The idea that faith regenerates is absurd on the face of it. The uncreated, the dead, and the unborn can do nothing – not even exercise faith. As a matter of fact, the Scriptures teach that faith itself, which is a *product* of regeneration (or quickening), is a *gift* (Ephesians 2:8, 9). A gift is something that another presents to you. It is neither earned by nor provided by oneself.

So regeneration is an act of God, performed solely by Him upon those to whom He determines to show His love. But is sanctification, which regeneration makes possible, *like* regeneration in this respect? As in regeneration, is the believer passive during the process of sanctification? The answer is, "Most certainly not!" Regeneration – the imparting of life, giving birth, creating anew – is described by expressions that also indicate that once one gets on the lee side of regeneration, the now regenerate Christian surely will become active. Life implies growth and all of the activities that encourage it. Resurrection implies newness of lifestyle that will take the place of the old one. Creation implies fresh outlooks, responsibilities, and endeavors! All three terms imply purposes to achieve. There is a reason for regeneration! Why should there be such changes in the

---

1. These are the three principal images or figures of speech under which regeneration is set forth in Scripture. All three, in one way or another, speak of imparting life or "quickening."

believer if there is nothing for him to do with the new orientation and capabilities that he has received? It simply doesn't compute.

Despite views that teach otherwise, the Bible sets forth sanctification as a process (not an act) in which three forces, the Spirit, His Word, and the regenerated saint, all *work together* to bring about change. It is vital to understand this essential fact and to keep all three of these forces in a harmonious and complementary relationship. None of them must be pitted against the others, as some who hold other views often do. Rather, it must be understood that every attempt to eliminate or minimize one or more of the three leads to failure in living and in counseling. It is precisely *because* of the tight interrelationship of the three elements in sanctification that the counselor gets involved. He helps the Christian to bring into play all three elements so that the process moves forward as God intended. The counselor, therefore, must understand each of the parts played in the process of sanctification by the Spirit, the Word, and the believer.

Obviously, the biblical counselor is not involved in the act of regeneration, in which the Spirit *alone* transforms the person. But now that the person has been transformed, his new orientation (toward God and righteousness) and his new capacity (to think and do those things that please God) bring that new person himself prominently into the picture. He must *use* the new ways of thinking and living that regeneration has made possible for God's glory. They must not be allowed to lie dormant. It is the counselor's task, among others, to help the counselee to recognize, understand, and draw upon the new resources that he possesses. One of the major reasons some counseling falls short is the failure of the believer to understand, call upon, and integrate all the resources that God has provided for him to encounter, fight, and defeat sin in his life.

Counselors and counselees must reject every form of "quietism," both because of its unbiblical nature and because of the frustration and defeat it occasions.[1] Often connected with quietism is the concept of a "second work of grace," the "baptism (or filling) of the Spirit" or a "second blessing." These and other names are used to describe an instantaneous act of God at some point subsequent to regeneration,[2] by which the believer is raised to a "higher plane." The way into this seemingly glorious, cloud nine experience differs according to each system. The Christian may be instructed to follow a prescribed set of steps. Or he may be informed that it is by yielding, or by making a *total*[3] consecration, that instantaneous or entire sanctification will take place. The result of taking this action (or commitment to *in*action), we are told, is either to attain to a state where one may have greater "victories" over temptation and sin, or to attain to *"entire* sanctification." The latter "result" may be presented either as a total eradication of

---

1. *Quietistic* teachings all stress change through human *passivity.* The pursuit of holiness through active obedience to Scripture is often derisively labeled "activism," and Christians are carefully steered away from it. Rather, a quietistic formula (they do not all agree) is offered instead. Quietistic "techniques" for change consist primarily in "letting go and letting God," as some have expressed it. The idea is that the more the Christian does, the more harm he will do and the less he will grow. To the extent to which *he* becomes actively involved in his sanctification, it will fail. This, we are told, is because self is the problem. Every effort by the self – even the transformed self – must be rejected and eschewed. Instead, the believer must let *God* effect change *for* him, *instead* of him. This passive approach, in effect, denies the transforming work of the Spirit in regeneration, or at best makes it pointless. If regeneration accomplishes any transformation at all, it is merely to open the believer to the further work of the Spirit. It is only as he "rests," "abides," or depends more and more on God to do what he cannot (and must not attempt) that he is sanctified. Biblical teaching, however, stresses the renewal of the believer in such a way that *he* may actually please God by what he thinks and does. His new abilities and capacities are to be *used,* not avoided.

2. Although some believe that it may happen concomitant with regeneration.

3. Avoid any belief that requires *total* or *absolute* "surrender" (or some similar term; see also Andrew Murray's book entitled *Absolute Sur-*

sin or as an ability to do everything in "perfect love."[1] "Mistakes"[2] are still thought to be made, or it is taught that all *willful* sin is eradicated (inadvertent sin, it seems, does not count). Sometimes, in spite of the perfectionism involved in such teaching, the need for growth is postulated. But such growth is usually not thought of in terms of the putting off/putting on dynamic of Colossians 3 and Ephesians 4, where *sinful living* is *being replaced* daily by righteousness living. On the whole, there is a wide range of similar beliefs that fall into the same basic scheme of quietistic and/or instantaneous sanctification, which differ only in minor details. But regardless of how these details differ, they have one thing in common: for them, sanctification is not a matter of on-going struggle, active pursuit, obedience, or growth; rather, it comes in some other way – usually in some crisis experience.

In these beliefs, passages having to do with our *status* before God that refer to what John Murray called "definitive

---

*render*). The fallacy of a system that teaches the need for this sort of experience is that *total freedom from sin or its power* supposedly is the result of total "yielding." This is begging the question. If the system were consistent, its adherents would declare a *total* commitment to be impossible until one had already attained perfection (that is, *total* sinlessness). But then, of course, commitment leading toward sanctification would not be needed! The fact is, since no believer is free from sin (I John 1:8), a *total* commitment (the phrase used by Charles Solomon and others) is impossible. James 3:2, 8, states, "All of us stumble in many ways. If anybody doesn't stumble in speech, he is a perfect man... but no human being anywhere is able to tame the tongue." While one may make progress in bridling the tongue, the problem of an unruly tongue (as well as the many other ways in which James says we *all* stumble) is a problem we shall face so long as we are in this present body.

1. John Wesley's terminology for sinlessness.

2. Sins are either toned down and called "mistakes," or the list and type of sins is shrunk to those of an easily "avoidable" nature and number. Either way, in order to justify this view, the lifestyle is viewed as free from sin by greatly minimizing sin. In helping those who shorten the list of sins, counselors will have to emphasize that a sin is doing what God forbids and/or failing to do what He requires.

sanctification" (the setting aside of a person to God at the time of justification) are wrongly applied to the post-regenerate, post-justified believer. As I have indicated previously, this status before God serves as the goal toward which our daily sanctification is to progressively move.[1] Definitive and progressive sanctification – what is on the record and what must be done to live up to that record – are obviously closely associated, but it is an error to equate rather than distinguish them. Definitive sanctification verses declare that "in Christ," by God's act, we have been set apart to Him as His "saints." We do not go on daily becoming saints. But we must work at becoming saintly. Even the failing, sinning Christians in Corinth are called "saints" because they were by God's act set apart from others as His people. In such passages, the word "sanctified" is used in a sense nearly identical to "justified."[2] Passages referring to progressive sanctification, on the other hand, refer to struggle, growth, and the pursuit and attainment of more and more holiness in daily living.

This book is principally concerned with progressive sanctification. We have seen that there are three elements that combine to bring about more and more holiness in the regenerated believer. The *Spirit* uses His *Word* as He enables the *believer* in faith and practice to obey it. It is each of these three elements that we now must consider in turn.

---

1. See also Colossians 3:1–9, where considering oneself raised into heaven "together with Christ" is used as an incentive to holy living!

2. I am not saying that the words *mean* the same thing, but that, from different approaches, they *refer* to the same thing.

## Chapter Five
## The Spirit, Sanctification, and Counseling

What the Spirit of holiness[1] begins, He continues and (ultimately) completes.[2] But it is that period between the beginnings of holiness and the believer's perfection that we shall consider in this chapter.

Peter unequivocally says to his readers that you were "chosen according to the foreknowledge of God the Father, that *by the Spirit's sanctification* you may obey..." (I Peter 1:2, emphasis mine). Here, God's electing intention for the believer is obedient living.[3] And it is is "by"[4] the sanctification that the Spirit produces that one "obeys" God's commands. That one verse contains all three of the elements that we mentioned at the close of the previous chapter: the Spirit, the Word (the only place where the will of God that must be obeyed can be found[5]), and the regenerate believer (who does the obeying). But notice the "setting apart" (or sanctification) is said to be the Spirit's" sanctification. He is the one Who primarily produces it. It is therefore rightly called "His."

He is the One Who "carried along" the writers of Scripture, so that what they wrote was, at the same time, precisely what God wanted them to say and what they

---

1. Romans 1:4. The phrase "Spirit of holiness" means "the Spirit from Whom holiness comes," and shows the absolute necessity of the Spirit's work not only in regeneration but also subsequent to it in sanctifying those He regenerates.

2. The spirits of just (justified) men are "made perfect" (complete) in glorification, Hebrews 12:23. Obviously, the context (Hebrews12:22, 23) makes it clear that men are made perfect in (and not before) the "heavenly Jerusalem."

3. See also Ephesians 2:10, where Paul says that God's attention for Christians is to "create" them "for good works."

4. That is, "by" in the sense of "by *means* of." Here, the Greek *en* is used instrumentally.

5. For an in-depth treatment of this assertion, see my book *The Christian's Guide to Guidance.*

themselves wanted to say. The words of the Bible can be called the Spirit's speech (as the writer of Hebrews calls them in passages such as Hebrews 3:7; 10:15, 16). So the Spirit brings about sanctification by providing the Standard (the Bible) by which progress in holy living may be judged. And according to I Corinthians 2:9 through 12, it is the Spirit Who opens the eyes and the ears of the regenerate believer to understand that Word. Such matters are incomprehensible (even "foolishness;" I Corinthians 1:18) to "modern day leaders" of the world who do not have the Spirit within them (I Corinthians 2:8). Moreover, God has poured the Spirit into our hearts (Romans 5:5) in order to motivate us by the love that is "producing in us what pleases Him" (Hebrews 13:21).[1] It is by the Spirit that the "new person" in Christ is being renewed in such a way as to produce the "full knowledge that is in keeping with the image of his Creator." (Colossians 3:10).

What is it that the Spirit is doing to renew us? God the Father is *enabling* the regenerate believer to "walk by the Spirit" as He fights against the "desires of the flesh" (Galatians 5:16).[2] And He does this by *replacing* the works of the flesh (Galatians 5:19–21) with His "fruit" (Galatians 5:22–24). Paul's argument is that, having been granted newness of life "by the Spirit," we should also "walk by the Spirit" (Galatians 5:25).[3] To walk by the Spirit means to live

---

1. See also Philippians 2:13. God is working "in us" through the Spirit, Who dwells within us. When we were baptized with the Spirit (I Corinthians 12:13) at regeneration, He took up residence in us for the purpose of equipping us "with every good thing for doing His will" (Hebrews 13:21a).

2. Paul is speaking about the habits and patterns of thinking and doing developed before regeneration that are brought over into the post-regenerate life. These habits desire to continue and to gain ascendancy in the new life. For details about this problem and the Spirit's solution to it, see my discussion of "flesh" in Romans 6 and 7 found in *Winning the War Within*.

3. Because we have "crucified the flesh with its passions and desires" *by the Spirit* in definitive sanctification ("If we live [have been

according to His Word, His wisdom, and His power.

How does the Spirit help Christians to do this? By "renewing" (literally, "rejuvenating," Ephesians 4:23) them in "the attitude" of their "minds." This new orientation, as we have called it earlier in this book, has to do with one's *attitude* toward God and righteousness as well as his attitude toward himself and his own thoughts and ways. The attitude previous to regeneration and the reception of the Holy Spirit is toward one's own desires, ideas, and ways, while it is *away from God, His thoughts, and His ways.* The new "attitude of mind" is *toward God and His righteousness.* This changed "attitude" and ability to comprehend God's Word enables one who has been "created" anew "in God's likeness with righteousness and holiness that come from the truth," to "put off lying..." and so forth (Ephesians 4:24–25). The Spirit works through, not apart from, the new attitudes and capacities of the regenerate believer. That is one reason for "renewing" him.

The new "attitude" toward *truth* that the Spirit has created in the regenerated believer is a craving to learn and to do what God says in His Word. It is clear that sanctification takes place through a "knowledge of the truth" (cf. John 17:17: "Sanctify them by Your truth; Your Word is truth," NKJV). Notice, also, that "the new person" is being "renewed in such a way as to produce full knowledge that is in keeping with the image of his Creator" (Colossians 3:10). According to Ephesians 4:24, the "new person" is "created in God's likeness with righteousness and holiness [sanctification] that *come from the truth*" (emphasis mine). Once again, it is the Spirit Who provides and Who enables one to believe and follow the "truth." It is He who progressively sanctifies the person as he comprehends truth and lives it in accordance with Titus 1:1: where Paul writes that

---

brought to spiritual life] by the Spirit;" Galatians 5:25), we are to "walk" by the Spirit in daily life (progressive sanctification). See Jesus' call to discipleship in which we are called to "take up the cross" (i.e., to crucify "the desires of the flesh" as we "deny" our own desires; Matthew 16:24).

"the full knowledge of the truth …is in the interest of godliness." In other words, the two-fold problem set forth by Isaiah (55:8, 9) is being solved by the Spirit through the Word that He inspired. The Spirit revealed the truth of the Word (I John 2:27) and, as believers study and apply it in life, the Spirit inculcates its teachings in their attitudes, minds, and walk. According to I John 4:6 and 5:7, the Spirit is called "the Spirit of truth." Because of the Spirit's presence and work in us (I John 4:13) we are said to be "of the truth" (I John 3:19) and are urged to love not only by word, but also by "deed and truth." So it is "the teachings of God's Spirit" (in Scripture) that Christians are able to "investigate spiritually" – that is, by the Spirit Who dwells within (I Corinthians 2:14).

Now, of course, it is possible for Christians to behave "like fleshly people" (I Corinthians 3:3). What does that mean? He is speaking about believers who, because they fail to appropriate their resources as they should (see also Philippians 4:19), are "walking like men without the Spirit" (I Corinthians 3:3). In other words, believers ought to be walking in accordance with God's will because they are men *with* the Spirit! That is to say, when relying on His Word and following it by His power, they have the knowledge and the ability to walk in His will.

So Paul's prayer for the Colossians is that they "may be filled with the full knowledge of His [God's] will in all spiritual wisdom and understanding" (Colossians 1:9). *Spiritual* wisdom and understanding is the wisdom and understanding that the Spirit provided in the Bible and that He enables believers to understand and live by. This wisdom and understanding were provided not simply to "fill" their heads, but also to enable them "to walk in a way that is worthy of the Lord, pleasing him in everything" (Colossians 1:10). And he continued, praying that they "be empowered with every sort of power" to do so (v. 11). A

At the conclusion of that first chapter of Colossians, Paul sums up everything in this passage concerning the ministry of the Word by saying, "which is Christ in you, the hope of glory, Whom we announce, counseling every person and teaching every person as wisely as possible" (Colossians 1:28). This leads us now to turn to the human element in the matter (that of the counselee and the counselor).

## Chapter Six
# The Human Factor in Sanctification

Some years ago I was invited to speak at a Keswick conference in Trinidad. Halfway through the conference the leaders drew me aside to talk. They said, in effect, "What you are teaching is different from what we have heard before. You are saying that we can *do* something about our problems." They were amazed at the notion and pleasantly relieved that they did not have to sit by, idly "resting" or incessantly "yielding," while waiting for God to do something in them and for them. They misunderstood Romans 12:1:

> I urge you then, brothers, because of these mercies from God, to present your bodies as living, holy, pleasing sacrifices to God, which is the reasonable way to serve Him in worship.

They had been taught that "yielding" (or "presenting") one's body meant surrendering it to God to do as He pleased with it, and that, as a result, they would not have to do anything themselves. God would give them a higher life as the result of "presenting" (or yielding). It had not worked, they told me, and they were surprised to discover (as I showed them) that Romans 1:1 was but an echo of Romans 6:13 through 19, where the expressions "present your bodily members" (v. 13), "present yourselves" (v. 16) and "present your members" (v. 19) first occur. I went on to make the point that in these passages in Romans 6, the bodily members were to be presented "as instruments of righteousness" to be used in "obedience" as God's slaves who are "to bring about sanctification" (v. 13, 16, 19). In other words, God expected them to use their bodies to serve Him in His righteous ways, thereby also bringing about their "sanctification" and its "fruit" (v. 22).

This passage pictures someone who had been a slave to sin, obeying its commands and thereby using the members of his body to further unrighteousness, switching allegiance to God as his new Master. Just as he had used his body in the service of sin, he is now to use it in the service of God and righteousness. Surely before conversion he did not "rest" or "yield" to sin in some quietistic manner! Nothing of the sort was in Paul's mind. Nor did anything like it flow from his pen. The Christian is to present himself to God as His slave who is willing to "obey from the heart the pattern of teaching to which he was handed over" (v. 17). His task is now "to bring about sanctification" as he once brought about "lawlessness" (v. 19). There is nothing but activity, service, and obedience in the passage!

So there is a part that the believer must play in his sanctification. That is clear. Indeed, if there were nothing he could do, if he had no part, counseling would be useless. All one could do, were this the case, would be to urge the Christian who is in trouble to yield again – this time more completely or more sincerely. And when this failed, as indeed it would, the message to him would be the same! After a while, as these Trinidadian believers discovered, their hopes would flag; their discouragements would mount. They would soon adopt one of two attitudes: they would say "What's the use?" Or, on the other hand, in self-deceit, they might pretend to themselves (and perhaps to others) that they were living life "on a higher plane."

Every biblical counselor must recognize that his message should be quite different from that of the quietist. While he will in no way diminish the emphasis upon the necessary work of the Spirit that I have highlighted in the previous chapter, neither will he play down the part of the counselee himself. Everywhere in Scripture, the Christian is commanded to obey God's Word. To intimate that he may do so apart from the Spirit and the Word is the serious error that the quietist thinks we fall into. And indeed, if any of us call upon a counselee to struggle with his problems in his own wisdom and power, we certainly fall into the error of which the quietists accuse us. But that is not the teaching of those who belong to the nouthetic movement because that is not the teaching of the Bible.

Now, contrary to the quietist's ideas of our counseling, we teach that counselees should be confronted with the commands of God's Word and called upon to obey them (Matthew 28:20) "from the heart"[1] (Romans 6:17) *by the enabling power* of the Spirit *according to,* and *never apart from,* the Bible. Thus all three elements in sanctification are to be brought into play in biblical counseling.

I will not take the time here to develop this point further, since in my book *The Theology of Counseling,* chapter fifteen,[2] I have discussed in depth the believer's "Pursuit of Fruit," which is encouraged in I Timothy 6:11 and II Timothy 2:22. The interesting thing is that while in Galatians 5 Paul stresses that fruit is the result of the Spirit's work, in these two passages in the pastorals he stresses the part that the Christian plays in pursuing it. Neither passage is to be used to the exclusion of the other. In one context, the need to emphasize dependence on the Spirit may be paramount; in others, there will be a need to stress responsibility. But one must be careful never to give the impression that what is said is all there is to the story. Paul never did. He was able to say both that the Spirit produces the fruit and that the Christian himself must pursue it – without contradiction.

That there is abundant biblical data on this point is clear. There is no commandment given to the Holy Spirit (or to "Christ in us"); all commands are given to the Christian. It is *he,* not anyone else, who must obey. You will find Christians who have been taught that the Spirit (or Christ in them) will do everything if they simply yield. If they are still confused after hearing an explanation of the biblical teach-

---

1. That is, genuinely, as whole persons; not by pharisaical, outward conforming.

2. See also my book *Maintaining The Delicate Balance in Christian Living,* where I discuss the need for the biblical balance between human and the divine elements.

ing, you might give them the following homework assignment, which I have found helpful in such cases. Send them home to go through the book of I Corinthians (or any fairly long New Testament book) noting on paper every time the Holy Spirit (or Christ in you) is commanded to do something and every time that the believer is commanded to do something. When they return with no notes about verses that command the Spirit or Christ to do anything and notes that show every command is given to the believer, it helps to drive home your point.

It is important, then, to develop from the Bible the doctrine of human responsibility for sanctification. But always make it clear that part of that responsibility is to call upon God for the wisdom and strength to obey (as Paul did in Colossians 1:9–14). These two qualities come from the Spirit using His Word – to which subject we now must turn our attention.

## Chapter Seven
# Sanctification and the Word

Jesus' words, "Sanctify them by the truth; Your Word is truth" (John 17:17) say it all. Yet it seems some have difficulty believing it. Sanctification does not take place apart from the Word of God, the Bible. There is no hope of spiritual growth for those who depend on hunches, promptings and checks in the spirit, feelings, and the like. Because I have dealt with this matter in *The Christian's Guide to Guidance*, I shall do little more here than to note the danger of turning outside of the Word of God to such supposed means of instruction in solving counseling problems. The emphasis on subjective, experience-oriented teaching always leads astray.

But let me ask one question: When God has provided such clear-cut direction in His Word, why is it that Christians ignore it and turn to other supposed sources of help? We should be so delighted to think that God has provided this inerrant guide to life and godliness that we ought to spend as much time as we can delving into it. Think of it: the living God, the Creator, and Sustainer of all things, has condescended not only to send His Son to die for our sins to save us but also to give Christians a wonderful Book with all that we need to serve and love Him and our neighbors (See also II Peter 1:3; II Timothy 3:17)! What foolishness, not to say ingratitude, on the part of those who fail to obtain the help that God has provided and that they need, and as a result, lead miserable lives, hurt His cause, and disgrace His Name – all because they neglect to study and appropriate the truths of the Bible! It is almost unthinkable!

Counselors, if you fail to stress the utter importance of the Scriptures as the third element in furthering the process of sanctification, you are equally remiss. There is no excuse to allow (not to mention encourage) counselees to turn anywhere else for help in sanctification. When you detect a dependence by counselees upon outside sources of "help," it is your duty to help them to see that this is one, if not the principal, reason that they have gotten into trouble. Your task, in such cases, is not only to help them straighten out the presenting problem, but also to help them with the greater problem – their failure to use Scripture to frame their lives. Having helped a counselee out of his difficulty, it is then worthwhile to take an extra session or two to discuss the whole matter of God's Standard for faith and practice – the Bible – and how to get help from it.

Obviously, you do not have time to teach a course on biblical interpretation, application, and implementation in counseling sessions, but you ought to take the time to strongly urge them to learn all they can about such matters. It was because of these time limitations despite the need for such study that I wrote the book *What to Do on Thursday*. This book not only takes the reader through a course in interpretation, application, and implementation, but also does so in a unique way. It does not simply set forth abstract principles without showing the reader how to move from the problem to the biblical solutions. Rather, it starts with the problem (encountered on Thursday – or any other day) and leads to the Bible, showing how to locate, interpret, and use the passages that are pertinent to the problem. If you do not have some better way of helping counselees to "get into" the Scriptures in a similar or better way, I urge you to examine this volume to see whether or not it is exactly what you need to give to counselees. At any rate, it is necessary to help counselees learn how to use the Bible to solve problems, or they will be back in the counseling room in six months or sooner!

All that I have said about turning to supposed "help" from outside of the Bible so far applies every bit as much to those counselors and counselees who believe that the principles and practices of pagan counselors can aid in the sanctifying process. I have already noted John 17:17 at the head of this chapter. In that verse we are told that it is truth that sanctifies. But notice, the source of truth is said to be

God's Word.

God spoke His Word audibly and in dreams and visions in times past, and He sent His Son Jesus Christ as the embodiment of that Word (Hebrews 1:1–3; John 1:1). But the revelation of truth which He has given to us was completed with the writing of the last book of the New Testament.[1] And the revelation of every other sort mentioned above is dependent upon what He has revealed about it in the Scriptures. So our one source of special revelation is the Bible. Every counselor must come to this conviction and counsel in the light of it or he should stop calling himself a "biblical" counselor.

In spite of what I have just said, there are those who seek to integrate biblical truth with the fallible theories and the ideas of men. That is sad, not to say harmful. When God's pristine, perfect truth is diluted by the addition of the pagan ideas of men, whose thoughts are not God's thoughts and whose ways are not His (remember Isaiah 55:8, 9), the "help" that is offered is seriously weakened. Often the "help" is no help at all. We find so-called "biblical" counselors reasoning from human wisdom about how God will permit divorce for reasons not given in the Bible. We find them offering advice about child rearing that is contrary to what God teaches. We find counselors excusing counselees from responsibility for sinful behavior because of their upbringing. And the list of aberrations from biblical truth go on and on. It is time to stop this! Are you one who has been unfaithful to God's Word, seeking to find truth elsewhere?

Now, don't tell me that "all truth is God's truth." That old weary argument is threadbare. Everyone agrees about that slogan. But the corollary is that "all error is the devil's error." How can you tell which is which? Obviously, there must be a standard by which truth can be discerned. The

---

1. I have dealt with the cessation of special revelation in my book *Signs and Wonders in the Last Days* (q.v.).

Bible itself is that Standard. So it turns out that all paths lead the Christian back to the Bible.

But equally telling is the fact that God's special revelation – revelation about life and godliness – is revealed only in the Bible. There the Christian counselor can find *"all things* necessary for life and godliness" (II Peter 1:3–6 [emphasis mine]). And, according to that passage, the things that make the believer's life "active"[1] and "fruitful" (v. 8) are the biblical "promises" of God through which one may become a "partaker of the divine [i.e., divinely-given] nature" (v. 4) that enables him to escape from "the corruption that is in the world." In other words, these promises *separate* one from it, or, we may say, sanctify him. He must "make every effort" to bring the qualities mentioned in the passage into his life (v. 5).

In his letters, the Apostle John warns about the many false teachers who seek to lead Christians astray. In discussing this matter in his letter to the "elect lady," he wrote,

> Watch yourselves, that you don't lose that which you have worked for, but rather that you may receive a full reward. Everybody who goes beyond, and doesn't remain in the teaching of Christ, doesn't have God. The one who remains in the teaching has both the Father and the Son (II John 8, 9).

Now, there are several facts to note in that statement. First, there are those who would lead Christians away from what the apostles taught about Christ. That temptation has continued until today. Second, those Christians who were advancing in sanctification by "working" for it could lose something of the "reward" they might otherwise have had by succumbing to the temptation to "go beyond" the apostolic message. Note, incidentally, the "active" human element that John says is involved! Third, these false teachings came from people who did not "have God" as Father and Son. Fourth, the one who remains in apostolic teaching

---

1. N.B., quietistically-inclined counselor!

(which today is found only in the Bible) demonstrates by his continuing fidelity to the teaching that he "has both the Father and the Son." Finally, the problem is stated in these terms: the temptation is to "go beyond."

Go beyond what? The text makes that clear: the temptation is to "go beyond" the "teaching" (v. 9). It is interesting that the one who goes beyond is viewed as no longer "remaining" in the apostolic teaching (now found in the New Testament). It is not a matter of simply *diluting* by adding to, but a matter of *abandoning* by going beyond. Every counselor who turns to the theories of ungodly psychologists and other counselors places himself in the position of going beyond the biblical teaching about life and godliness. If he allows his counselees to seek counsel outside Scripture, he fails to warn them as John did.

In either case there is the possibility of losing one's reward. Rather, the counselor should aim at the "full reward" for both himself and his counselees. To play around with the theories of men, rather than adhere to the truth of God, is to place oneself and one's counselees in the way of serious danger. John is quite strong on this point: "Everybody who goes beyond, and doesn't remain in the teaching of Christ, *doesn't have God*" (emphasis mine). It may be that some of those in the church calling themselves "Christian counselors" who "go beyond" the truths of the Bible that are designed to sanctify are not truly Christians at all. I have known those who began to do what they called Christian counseling who, after dabbling in all sorts of beliefs other than the Bible, became enamored with them, left the Bible behind, and became full-fledged non-Christian counselors. They now make no pretense about being "biblical" or "Christian" in their counseling. Counselor, are you tempted to adopt non-Christian teachings? Counselee, does the counselor from whom you seek help take his directions from the Bible? Or does he "go beyond"?

There are many other passages to which we might turn in showing how the Bible, along with the Spirit and the counselee himself, all play a part in sanctification. Remember, each must be given its proper due. To state it simply, the counselor must urge the counselee to think and do what God, in Scripture, says he ought to, by the power of the Spirit working through the Word to inform and enable him through prayer. At every point, the counselor should set the example of these things for his counselee. Then, and then alone, will you see people growing by grace (II Peter 3:18).

## Chapter Eight
# Let's Talk about Counseling

So far, I have spent the lion's share of the space in this book discussing sanctification. That was important since it was necessary to establish clearly what we are talking about. I have mentioned counseling largely in an incidental way. It is time to zero in on some of the major issues in counseling that are related to sanctification.

I want to spell out again, from a different angle, two reasons that a thorough understanding of sanctification and its place in counseling should be of importance to counselors. First, counseling usually begins when the process of sanctification comes to a halt or is seriously impeded by some problem. In such times, counseling is specifically intended to assist the progress of sanctification. That is why counseling comes into play. Second, the matters with which counselors are concerned in counseling are sanctification matters. For these reasons, the counselor should not be indifferent to issues having to do with Christian growth. Because both of these issues are of such great importance, I intend to devote a chapter to each.

To begin with, an individual usually needs counseling because of some factor that has blocked the normal growth process. It is then that he seeks help from a counselor or others urge him to do so. Often, it is a wife who urges her husband to go to counseling with her; less frequently it is the other way around. Sometimes some interested party such as a parent, a child, a relative, or a friend encourages counseling. And then there are institutional influences – a Christian school or some other organization may insist on counseling for a student or a worker. And last but certainly not least, a pastor may initiate the process by going to the person or persons involved and offering his services.

These persons, and perhaps others as well, advise people to seek counseling because they detect something wrong about the attitudes, the words, or the behaviors of the one whom they encourage to receive counseling. In effect, though they may not put it in these terms, they perceive that their Christian brother or sister has stopped growing, that the process of sanctification in one way or another is stymied. They may see a marriage that is faltering. They may sense an attitude of depression, defeat, or dismay. They may encounter a brother who has ceased using the means of grace (Bible study, prayer, church attendance, etc.). They may catch another in sin (Galatians 6:1); they may suspect that there is a problem of some sort and, having confronted the person, discover that they were right. All of this ought to be done out of loving concern (though, sadly, that does not always happen). But each of these reasons for encouraging someone to seek counsel is based on the idea (not always understood or expressed as such) that the person has ceased growing in his Christian life as he should. That is to say, the process of sanctification has come to a halt or has been greatly set back.

So we see that sanctification is the counselor's biblical, immediate concern. The counselor should, from the very start, consider his counselee's situation and problem differently than the non-Christian or integrationist counselor. He should always be thinking about counseling problems *in terms of sanctification.*

What does that mean? Among other things it means that he will want to know about the counselee's growth patterns prior to the onset of the problem(s). He will want to know how the counselee views his problem – does he see it merely as a sad thing, a tragedy, a difficulty to be overcome, or a matter to be settled with others? Or does he see it as a setback in his growth by grace in serving and honoring God? That is to say, does he think of the problem in terms of sanctification or not? The counselor is concerned about the way in which the counselee thinks because often he must turn the counselee's thinking and behavior from other concerns to focus on sanctification. Until both the counselor and the counselee think in those terms, the counseling will have a wrong focus and will go nowhere, at least as far as biblical growth out of sin and into righteousness is concerned.

The counselor will be concerned to discover two things: how these problems impede the process of sanctification and what measures must be taken to get the individual on the sanctification track once again. It is this orientation toward sanctification that makes biblical counseling unique. Other counselors do not think in those terms. Christian counselors, when counseling properly, always do. Their concern is not about counseling *per se*, it is not a concern with problems or even extricating counselees from them; rather, it is a concern about turning the counselee's thinking and ways from sin and toward righteousness.[1]

In this chapter we are not so much interested in what to do about problems of sanctification as in asking how to think about what is wrong. The answer to that question could take many forms, but if sanctification is uppermost in the counselor's thinking, the many issues involved in understanding the counselee's problem will coalesce. That is not to say that complex matters will be oversimplified. But just as a farmer has a farming viewpoint to which he relates all else, so the counselor relates the many aspects of problems that emerge in data gathering[2] to this one issue: how each aspect impinges upon sanctification. The importance of seeing the central place of sanctification in all that is done in counseling cannot be overstated. Sanctification is the thread that runs through all of counseling.

So it is important to foster this outlook in one's counselees from the outset. Whenever a counselee wanders from the importance of pleasing God by spiritual growth on to some other trail, bring him back with words such as, "That may all be true, but how does what you are now talking about help you to grow and love God and your neigh-

---

1. Remember Isaiah 55:8, 9!

2. For a two-chapter discussion of data gathering, see *The Christian Counselor's Manual.*

bor?" A believer ought to respond favorably to such interrogations, so long as he does not use them as a way of avoiding issues. The idea is not to distract the counselee's attention from something he considers important; rather, it is to help him to view the matter in different terms, in a different context. It is to help him to see that God is involved in the problem and that the manner of understanding and dealing with the problem must be one that reflects that fact. And specifically, it is to help him view every matter from the perspective of how he may grow in his spiritual life and thereby honor God. Sanctification becomes the skewer on which the counselee impales all his problems. It is to give him a handle on the problems so that he can deal with them in a biblical manner.

It ought to be plain to every Christian counselor that his task is made possible by maintaining this sanctification emphasis. He need not go off in all directions, wondering where to begin or end. Instead, because he can hang everything on the sanctification issue, he can more easily determine what to do both in data gathering and in seeking solutions to the problems that he discovers. Indeed, keeping an eye firmly fixed on the goal of resuming and furthering sanctification in a counselee turns counseling into a valuable ministry that accords with the ongoing ministry of Christ's church, rather than making it something that is done outside of the context of church discipleship. It fits!

Understanding and maintaining this perspective in counseling enables the counselor to see that counseling is nothing in itself. It is but a means to an end. The end is the sanctification of the counselee. The *raison d'etre* for counseling is that the normal process of sanctification has stalled. Therefore, counseling is but a measure that is taken in order to break open the logjam and set the logs floating on their proper course. It diminishes the idea of being a "counselor" in the professional sense of the word – as, indeed it should! Counseling is a ministry of the church in which both ruling and teaching elders are to engage formally and officially, and in which all other members of the congregation are to engage informally and unofficially. The elder is a counselor *among other things*. There is no such thing as a professional counselor in the church other than an elder; and that is not his sole work. It is but one aspect of it. So counseling is diminished in the sense that it is but one of the many tasks in which those who perform other work are engaged. No one ought to hang out a shingle and set himself or herself up as a "professional" biblical counselor. Keeping the goal of sanctification in view helps counselors to remember this.

## Chapter Nine
## Common Territory

The close affinity between counseling and Christian living in general (and sanctification in particular) is natural. The two are concerned with and operate in common territory. The overlap of which I speak is natural, I say, because the materials of growth by grace and those of biblical counseling are the same. Problem solving, putting off the "old person" while putting on the new, and the pursuit of the Spirit's fruit, for instance, are common themes of both. Both may turn to I Peter 1:15 as their common mission statement: "Instead, as the One Who called you is holy, you yourselves must become holy in all your behavior." In short, the desire to be sanctified (separate) motivates both counseling and normal Christian living.

These common desires and goals are the reason non-Christian counseling cannot cut it. The materials used, as well as the concerns and the motivation of non-biblical counseling just cited, are foreign to the mission of the individual Christian and the Christian counselor. Indeed, non-Christian counselors strongly disapprove of sanctification, since, when you boil it down to its essentials to desire to be sanctified is a desire to become *different* – to be separate from others. Many consider this taboo.

Moreover, the goal of non-Christian counselors is to help counselees live up to the norm, to fit in with society. But the norm is that which the non-Christian culture of the day declares to be desirable.[1] The prevailing view among people today is relativism; that is, permission to believe whatever it is that you may wish to believe – except, of course, Christian teaching. One stated reason for this is Christianity's exclusiveness. It cuts across relativism, condemning it

---

1. See, for instance, Glasser, whose counseling expressly states that the goal is to make people fit in with whatever the prevailing culture may be.

out of hand. Christianity says that since there is but one God, we must know and serve Him His way; that there is no other. That got the apostles into trouble in their time. It was okay to add another god to your pantheon in Greco-Roman culture, but it was not okay to declare all other gods to be nothing more than idols. There is much the same attitude in our times.

So for Christians to turn to non-Christian counselors (or Christians who counsel according to their values) is to opt, in one way or another, for a relativistic solution to problems; one in which the counselee is "helped" by the counselor to blend into the culture. But Christians cannot do this since their beliefs are antithetical to the ambient culture.

Why is this so? How is it that the Christian must run against his culture? It is not out of a wish to be contrary. He would certainly prefer not to run headlong into the values of others around him – if they were values that the Bible allows him to accept. But they are not. Once again, the problem is this: God says that His ways and His thoughts are not those of the culture (Isaiah 55:8, 9). So in order to conform to God's ways and thoughts, the believer must reject the world's and accept God's.

I have said that Christian counseling is a part of the sanctification process: that the two occupy common ground. There are few cases that biblical counselors take on that do not to some extent involve the problem of breaking up logjams. I have briefly referred to this elsewhere. The problem is that the stream of sanctification has been clogged by unbiblical logs in the counselee's life. They must be broken up and sent downstream to the ocean. The reason logjams occur is that Christians do not always come for counseling help until serious jams have developed.[1]

The common territory occupied by Christian counseling and sanctification means that as the believer seeks to float

---

1. If they came earlier, much grief could be avoided and remedies would be simpler. Time complicates one's problem as more and more logs tend to pile up.

away the unseemly aspects of his character, these in turn resist change. Breaking up logjams is what counselors do. By their counsel they cause the normal flow of sanctification to resume.

Both the saint and his counselors, then, are different. No counselor but the Bible-believing one seeks to improve the progress of his counselee's sanctification. That's what true *Christian* counseling is all about – making people different, God's way, shaping them in ways and thinking that does not fit their culture. When the Christian deserted the enemy and surrendered to God, he pledged to do His will and become like Him. He was given a new name and a new status. His basic outlook changed, he acquired new capacities, he received the Holy Spirit as his constant Companion and Helper. And now he is involved in the process of becoming more like Christ, into Whose stature the Spirit is shaping him. All of this was God's gracious doing.

It is amazing that God declares wretched, redeemed sinners His special people. They are different because He has chosen to sanctify and make them His own (I Peter 1:2).[1] But God now expects them to live up to their new name and status. His purpose is to make them holy (set apart) in fact as well as in standing. And that is where all the problems appear. Sanctification, which involves the process of clearing the stream of sin, *itself* may lead to logjams. Those logs that have been firmly lodged over the years may resist removal and become the occasion for more and more logs to pile up. When a Christian finds himself unable or unwilling to break them loose, counseling becomes necessary.

Many balk at the very idea of becoming different. Old logs of conformity refuse to budge. Christians may be happy to be labeled "saints" and to know that they are

---

1. Peter tells his readers, "[You] are chosen according to the foreknowledge of God the Father, that by the Spirit's sanctification you may obey and be sprinkled by the blood of Jesus Christ." "Sprinkling" was a sacrificial means of purifying in which blood was sprinkled in order to sanctify.

headed for heaven, but *becoming* a saint is something else. Sainthood means becoming different, and becoming different means standing out from the crowd. *That* takes courage. And courage is precisely what many Christians lack. Even the apostles prayed for boldness (Acts 4:29).

Right here is where the counselor may find that counselees cause the logjam. Counselees appreciate the benefits and privileges associated with sainthood, but they are often less than enamored with the consequences and responsibilities associated with it. A person who is *set apart* is *noticed* – every bit as much as the two words printed in italics in this sentence. Because his behavior is different, it becomes noticeable. Peter mentions this fact when he writes, "it surprises others that you won't run with them in the same ruinous excesses, and they insult you" (I Peter 4:4). Notice, particularly, the last clause: "and they insult you." There's the rub. Sainthood in the closet, sainthood away from the prying eyes of the disapproving crowd, is okay. But that it should be noticed. No thanks.

Indeed, because sainthood is noticed, Christians often find themselves ridiculed and challenged about their behavior. Then, too, they become obligated to "defend the hope that is in [them] to everybody who asks [them]" (I Peter 3:15). Many counselees would rather not. And in the following verse, notice especially that he tells his readers that they will be "slandered" by "those who speak insultingly about your good behavior in Christ" (v. 16). Slandered for good behavior! Think of it. That is where many stumble. Counselees may be willing to make cosmetic changes that are not too obvious – but real heart changes that lead to saintly behavior? Behavior that leads to insults? Well… that's something else.

Christians get into trouble when they begin to live as they should and suffer consequences. Their number of close friendships may diminish. Since they live exclusive lives, they may find that others are more than happy to exclude them from theirs. They may find themselves becoming lonely, longing for companionship – especially if they neglect the fellowship of the church. They may become the butt of jokes, gossip, and slander. The more they conform to their name, *saints* ("the separated ones"), the more they become disassociated from those whose life-styles they may not follow.

On the other hand, though a Christian rightly refuses to become a part of the "Christian elite" who try to encase themselves in protective coverings to isolate themselves from the world around them, nevertheless a believer's neighbors and business associates, even family members, may avoid him. In some cases, the latter may even disown him. He is different, and people don't like it! The Christian who lives like he ought to is not different for difference's sake. He is different because he is becoming more like His Lord!

In dealing with counselees who are bogged down by these considerations, counselors must take a lovingly firm stance. They will distinguish those counselees whose growth in grace has been stunted by discouragement and loneliness from those who have ceased growing out of fear. The first may have sought to become holy but didn't know how to find new friends after being abandoned by old ones. The second class may have ceased growing as the result of reversion to old ways through capitulating to the pressures exerted by those around them.

The first group needs to be brought to repentance over the lack of gratitude that has caused their dispirited attitude, while the latter need to repent and forsake their straying ways. Both the disheartened, lonely counselee and the straying sheep must be helped to become more closely associated with other believers in the church.

The first class needs the encouragement through fellowship that the church can provide. The second needs the emboldening that comes from stronger believers standing with them. Both need the stimulation to "love and good deeds" about which we read in Hebrews 10:24 and 25. In all of this, the idea is not to flee into the Christian bubble, isolating oneself from contact with the world, but to gain the strength and courage that enable a believer to live a consistent Christian witness before all men.

Counselors will take these matters to heart and whenever they discover counselees who have become indolent or regressive will seek the correct response to their sin. They will help them appropriate the best resources in Christ and in His church. They will stress these resources since they recognize that they, themselves, cannot provide adequate assistance of the sort that the church surely can.[1]

Dealing with other sorts of problems, of course, will demand that counselors take appropriate measures. These problems, in addition to those just mentioned, also involve breaking up logjams and, in that respect, will not differ from those mentioned in other books (see *The Christian Counselor's Manual* and *How to Help People Change*). In speaking about breaking up logjams, I am not speaking of a specific sort of problem but rather of a problem that may become a complicating factor when another problem is not quickly resolved. For help with logjams, see my book *Critical Stages of Biblical Counseling* in which I deal with the matter more fully.

For now, the important matter to understand is that unresolved problems curtail sanctification and therefore must be dealt with. Sanctification cannot continue unabated when there is unrepentant sin and unresolved problems in one's life. The counselee is a whole person, and a breakdown in one area of sanctification affects the whole of it. He cannot, for instance, go on knowingly lying about some matter without grieving the Holy Spirit Who provides the power for sanctification. And he will avoid the

---

1. The problem here is that not every church is ready to offer help. The counselor may have to work with members in the church as well as with his counselees in order to achieve this. Or, in the worst scenario, he may have to advise that a counselee leave his church and unite with another that will provide help.

convicting efficacy of the Word and the preaching of the gospel as well. All of this leads to a setback of spiritual growth and sanctification. For this reason, the counselor must consider himself an agent in furthering the sanctification process. The territory is the same. When he understands this, he will add a dimension to his work that is unique among counselors by what he says and does in counseling. Truly Christian counseling, designed to assist in the counselee's sanctification, is unique. Clearly, the focus on sanctification in the counseling process is what makes it so.

## Chapter Ten
# Nouthetic Counseling Is Unique

At the conclusion of the previous chapter I mentioned one unique feature of Christian (or nouthetic) counseling: it is part of the sanctification process. There are very few cases that counselors face that do not involve breaking up logjams, as we have seen. That is because counselees do not come soon enough, so the initial problem is compounded by other problems. But it also may be because counselees follow unbiblical counseling, which only adds to the logjam. This underscores the idea that true Christian counseling alone can help one grow by grace. Biblical counsel has several features that should be explained further:

❖ *A Unique Clientelle.* Christian counselors have a unique clientele: they counsel only those who are capable of being sanctified. I discussed this earlier in the book. Because they are committed to following the premise that sanctification is (or ought to be) what we should achieve through counseling, they will not settle for doing anything else. They do not knowingly counsel unregenerate persons. Thus, the unique clientele grows out of the unique reason for counseling (not understood by others) – to further sanctification. But the same reason also leads to...

❖ *Unique Goals and Objectives.* All along the way, the counselor keeps biblical goals and objectives plainly in view. In addition to breaking logjams and permitting the process of sanctification to flow freely toward those goals and objectives, Christian counseling speeds up the process. It also focuses on helping counselees to avoid logjams in the future by adopting biblical lifestyles and pointing out areas in which sanctification has not yet begun or may be in danger of floundering. In examining his counselee's life, the counselor will often uncover such matters and can take preventive action that will help nip problems in the bud. In observing Christian counseling, one would also ascertain that

❖   *The Methods Are Unique.* For one thing, the counselor will pray and use his Bible. By introducing these elements into counseling he gives recognition to the obvious fact that he is not dependent upon his own wisdom and ingenuity. He is recognizing the presence of Another – with His supreme wisdom and power – in each counseling session. That unique fact in itself makes no small difference. Surely, it dramatically sets apart Christian counseling and its methods from all other counseling. In full accord with the fact of dependence on God and His Word, every method the believer employs in the course of counseling should grow out and be appropriate to Scripture at every point. Should a counselee ask, for instance, "Why do you assign homework? Why is it so necessary when I have gained such ground during the session?" The counselor must have a biblical response ready. In answering this question he might say something like the following: "Yes, you have moved forward in this session. But that is precisely why homework is necessary. You must now take the next step that is based on that success; you must add works to your faith. James clearly said, 'Faith without works is dead' (James 2:26). Moreover, fruit is supposed to follow repentance. As you make advances in repentance and faith, the assignments are calculated to help you to turn new understandings, new beliefs, and new commitments into fruit and works."

Because of the uniqueness of the purpose of Christian counseling, the counselor will not adopt the methods of non-Christian counselors. "Explain that, if you will," you may say. "Surely, you use talk, listening, and so on, as other counselors do – don't you?" Of course we do. But, you see, talk, listening, and other such elements common to all counseling (and indeed, to all communication) are not *methods*. They are *means*. Methods, in contrast, are means committed to the ends of a system. Ventilation, for instance, is a kind of talk that is designed to produce the results that Freud thought would solve his counselees' problems. Non-directive, reflective talk is a method used by Rogerians that is designed to accomplish the goal of drawing people's own ideas out. Rogerians would not use talk to give advice. As you can see, there is talk and there is talk.

Because those who developed each system described problems according to their presuppositions, they set goals that were intended to solve the problems in accordance with those prepositions. They then developed methods that were aimed at moving from the problem to the solution as follows:

Problem → Method → Solution

When descriptions of problems and solutions differ from system to system, methods must differ as well. Since sanctification is the Christian's goal (solution), the methods used by Christian counselors must lead to sanctification. Pagan methods are not designed for that purpose and will not achieve it. Those methods, therefore, must not be employed in Christian counseling. And along with the methods used by Christian counselors...

❖ *The Incentives Are Unique.* Christian counselors should not enter counseling full of fear or uncertainty. Rather, they should begin with great confidence. This confidence does not rest on their own wisdom or ability (though they ought to become as wise and discerning and able to use the Bible as is possible). It depends on the teachings and promises of God. A Christian counselor knows things that the non-Christian does not. He knows that the person who is in trouble is, in one way or another, involved in sin – either his own or another's. Sin is a quantity that other counselors are unfamiliar with and do not deal with. Yet it is the factor behind every problem that ever existed. Already the Christian counselor has an advantage; he understands man's basic problem.[1]

In addition to the fact that Christians have an inerrant source of knowledge about human beings from the Scriptures, they can also promise specific change in response to specific attitudes, commitments, and actions. Whatever God promises in the Bible, the counselor also may promise. He may say, for instance, "If you genuinely repent of the sin of homosexuality, you can live free from it. I tell you this on the basis of I Corinthians 6:9–11, where God's Word says that God enables people to do so."

Moreover, he knows that, in addition to the promise in II Peter 1:3 that he may find in Scripture "everything necessary for life and godliness," the counselee has dwelling within him the Holy Spirit, Who fights against sin and helps him desire and do those things that please God (cf. Philippians 2:13). This unique combination of the Word and the Spirit acting through the ministry of counseling to produce sanctification means that...

❖ *The Results Are Unique.* The two fundamental results of freeing the stream of sanctification from obstructing logjams is the honor of God and the blessing of His own. These two results can be found nowhere else other than in biblical counseling. If nouthetic counsel-

---

1. Sin is the broadest category since every problem – even organically based ones – find their cause in Adam's disobedience. Moreover, in the sins of each individual, and those that are committed against him, are included every sort of problem that is imaginable. Non-Christian counselors, and even many eclectic Christians, do not understand this. To focus on one of the problems occasioned by sin (the environment, training, organic difficulties, etc.) rather than on sin itself is a mistake.

ing is truly unique, why is it that some blunt its uniqueness by attempting to integrate it with other forms of counseling? Precisely because they do not believe that it is unique. It is the fact of the uniqueness of Christian counseling, then, that makes all the difference. This idea will gain acceptance only if its unique character is clearly related to its inseparable attachment to sanctification.

## *Chapter Eleven*
# Discipleship

Sanctification is a *daily* matter. We have seen that it is progressive rather than static. All those views that hold to some sort of instantaneous rise to a higher plane of living, either by one act or a series of steps, contradict the words of Jesus who declared that we must *take up the cross daily.* Were we to "arrive" in any sense at some point while we live in this life, Jesus' call would no longer be a daily necessity. Upon "arrival," the call would be dispensed with. Let's look at the exact wording of His call to discipleship:

> Then He said to all of them, "If anybody wants to come after Me, he must deny himself and *take up his cross daily* and follow me" (Luke 9:23, emphasis mine).

First we must come to an understanding of these words; only then can we look at their implications for sanctification and counseling. Understanding is important because this powerful verse is often misunderstood.

When Jesus used the words "come after me," He was issuing a call to discipleship. The call was different from what we do today when accepting someone into a school. We are too often interested only in academics. The catalogs spell out the content of courses. But it is notable that Jesus did not say merely "sit at My feet." A disciple is, literally, "a student, a pupil," but the idea that a student might merely learn facts that he could recite back to his teacher or replicate on a test was foreign to Hebrew education. One not only learned facts, he learned how to put them into practice (cf. the phrase in Matthew 28:20: "teaching them to *observe*" [emphasis mine]). And, note the important word of our Lord concerning discipling:

> A disciple isn't above his teacher; but everybody who has been thoroughly trained will be like his teacher (Luke 6:40).

Here, He makes the very important statement that effective discipling (thorough "training"), in the end, turns out students who not only *think* like their teacher, but also *become* like him. That was the goal that Jesus had in mind when He invited others to follow Him.[1] They would walk "with Him"[2] and observe what He did as well as learn from His lips what He taught. The whole Person was teaching whole persons.

The reintroduction of discipling into the teaching models of our Christian schools is a very crucial matter, but one that we cannot go into here.[3] For the moment we shall simply note that scholarship, biblically speaking, is a matter of *whole person learning*. It would, therefore, have everything to do with counseling for purposes of sanctification. Sanctification, as we have seen, is concerned with changing one's *ways* as well as his thoughts.

The second element we examine in the call to discipleship is the phrase "deny himself." The sacerdotalists take this to mean that one is to deny himself something (usually during Lent). That is precisely what Jesus was *not* saying. Leave out the word "something" and you will better understand Jesus' words. What He was saying is that one must deny him*self*. But what does it mean to deny one's self? Literally, in Greek the word *deny* means "say 'no.'" To deny self, then, is to say "no" to the desires of self that are out of accord with Christ's will. It is to reject one's own ways of thinking and doing (remember Isaiah 55:8, 9).[4]

Then there are the words "and follow me." That phrase sets forth the alternative to following one's self. The disci-

---

1. And others, at length, recognized that the training was effective: "Now when they saw the boldness of Peter and John and realized that they were uneducated laymen, they were surprised and recognized that they had been with Jesus" (Acts 4:13).

2. See also Mark 3:14: "He appointed twelve that they might be *with Him* and that he might send them out to preach" [emphasis mine].

3. For more on this, see my book *Back to the Blackboard*.

4. Certainly not those that accord with the Scriptures. See also Proverbs 3:5–7.

ple is one who will follow the desires, the thinking, and the walk of the Lord Jesus Christ. He is to say "no" to self, but "yes" to Christ.

Now comes the phrase "and take up his cross." That phrase also has been misconstrued by making it say, "I must take up some burden – an infirmity, the heartaches of a wayward child or a troublesome mother-in-law!" The cross was an instrument of *death*,[1] not merely a burden, and certainly not a lovely gold ornament to hang around the neck. To "take it up" was to carry it to the place where the burden-bearer would be crucified on it (remember the story about Jesus carrying His cross). So to take up one's cross meant to put one's self to death. Crucifixion was a sign of shame and ignominy. He is to die to the desires of his old self. In Colossians 3:5 Paul, possibly referring to Jesus' words, wrote: "So then, put to death the habits of the members of your earthly body." The expression "take up your cross" must not be toned down; it is powerful!

And, finally, we come to the word "daily." This emphasis on a day-by-day crucifixion and denial clearly sets forth the progressive nature of sanctification as over against the instantaneous view. The latter is false because of what Jesus describes as a daily effort[2] to put down sin in one's life and replace it with Jesus' wishes. The difference is vital.

Jesus knew that we would have difficulty following Him; that the sinful thoughts and ways that remain in the believer must be confronted regularly – indeed, on a daily basis. That does not mean that there will be no real victories and that, like AA participants, one must say to himself every day, "I am a drunk." No, according to I Corinthians 6:9 through 11, after listing a number of sins (including drunkenness), Paul says "Such were some of you." Notice the past tense. That is a very encouraging fact to realize. He

---

1. And not only death, but the death reserved for the worst sort of criminal. See also Philippians 2:6–8.

2. Notice the call involves a command, not some passive, quietistic "yielding."

raises an expectation that by following the call, one's life-style will change. The Believer *can* put sins behind him. He *can* learn new ways that please God. The disciple is not stuck with his sin. Take, for example, Peter's words:

> ...knowing that you weren't set free from the useless behavior patterns that were passed down from your forefathers, by the payment of a corruptible ransom like silver or gold, but with Christ's valuable blood, shed like the blood of a spotless and unblemished lamb (I Peter 1:18, 19).

Well, what does the emphasis upon "daily" denial and crucifixion mean then? Simply this: throughout this life, there will always be some sin remaining. Regardless of the amount of progress he may make, he will never eradicate all sin. Every day the believer will find that there is a struggle with sin, to which (as Jesus knew) we must die daily. There will always be ideas popping up that are wrong because they are not those of the One Whose faithful disciples we seek to become. He must hear Jesus' clear call and say "no" to the wrong ideas. And because all sin must be replaced with its biblical alternative, we must say "yes" to His ideas instead. The same must be true of the contrast between our sinful ways and His righteous ones. We must "just say no" – and mean it!

That the believer will make progress by faithful discipleship is inevitable, since it is the method by which one puts off the old lifestyle and puts on the new one. But it will happen only if he develops the discipling attitude that declares, "Today I will say 'no' to sin and 'yes' to righteousness." That sort of phrase might be printed as a motto on counseling materials and handouts.

Now, the Christian counselor who is bent on bringing about sanctification through his counsel will always stress the discipleship dynamic (which is the same as the put off/put on dynamic[1]). That is one reason it is virtually impossi-

---

1. See *The Christian Counselor's Manual* for details.

ble to do counseling in one session as some think. Usually, because many people today are undisciplined, the counselor must "ride herd" on his counselees over a period of time, checking up weekly on their progress. Ordinarily, it takes about six weeks of regular, consistent effort (40 days and 40 nights) to replace a habit. The habit of following the disciple's *daily* duty to say "no" to sin and "yes" to righteousness will develop only in time. To have to report on how well he is following this word from the Lord is helpful in establishing the new dynamic.

Moreover, throughout the weeks of counseling, the counselee's report on his progress in following Christ will help to define the exact nature his problems and whether or not what is happening in counseling will solve those problems. If, for instance, a counselee is struggling with lust, how well he is succeeding at concentrating on his work rather than lusting after the woman who works next to him at the office should emerge. How well another counselee is doing at holding her tongue when speaking to her husband will also appear. And as one learns to follow the Lord's call, he will see the progress for himself.[1]

Indeed, the counseling of daily denial and following will help the counselor to discover exactly where his counselee is failing. If there is change in what he is or isn't doing, it may be corrected before it is too late and it becomes a habitual error. And if the counselee is simply lapsing in his responsibility to follow Christ, it is then possible to encourage him to heed Jesus' call once more.

An entire series of counseling sessions might easily be conducted in terms of the call to discipleship, which we have seen is a call to sanctification. In each session, this question (or a similar one) may be considered: "Has sanctification been taking place this week? Let's examine it, to see what you have been doing or not doing." Then what-

---

1. Or the lack of it. There may be, as we said, logjams impeding progress.

ever is found, after being examined in the light of actual progress in sanctification, may be looked at from the perspective of what has or has not aided sanctification. If what is found neither leads to nor actually accomplishes sanctification, then measures may be taken to adapt the next week's homework to the situation.

The importance of discipleship-counseling as a way of evaluating progress cannot be over-emphasized. The reason this method of evaluating progress is so appropriate to counseling is that both focus on progress in sanctification. Jesus' discipling methodology of denial-and-following is but one way of saying what Paul and the other apostles described in their letters. The whole Bible teaches a regular, progressive work to be pursued by every disciple.

## Chapter Twelve
## Grow by Grace

The title of this book and the quotation from II Peter 3:18 on the title page set forth the theme of sanctification that I have been pursuing. In this chapter, I want to take the time to investigate Peter's words. Let me once more quote that verse, this time with the retranslation of but one word – grace:

> But grow by help and the knowledge of our Lord and Savior Jesus Christ.

This command follows a warning to "be on guard" not to be "led astray by the error of lawless persons" lest one lose his "own stability" (v. 17). The instability of untaught persons who "twist" the Scriptures (v. 16), Peter observes, is a major cause of instability in others. The way in which he puts it suggests that such Scripture twisting may be highly contagious. Untaught believers do not understand biblical truth and so lack stability; they may also cause others to lose their own stability. That, according to Peter, is why it is necessary to "grow by grace."

Of course, there are other reasons for growing by grace; some reasons – like the desire to please God – are even more fundamental than the one Peter raises. Nevertheless, this well-known exhortation to grow spiritually, presents one very important motive for growing and another exhortation for biblical counselors to heed. It is not a small matter when false teachers and false teaching twist God's Word, hindering spiritual growth by knocking the supports out from under counselees so that they too become unstable. Peter says that when the Scriptures are misinterpreted to mean what they were never intended to mean, they can be construed in a way that makes people question various aspects of the faith. And in some cases, the faith itself! When counselors fail to warn counselees, as Peter did – when they fail to expose and counter the false teaching (and sometimes confront those who teach it) as he did in his letters – they betray the Lord and fail to help their counselees as they should. This matter that we are about to consider, then, is important because false teaching may hinder sanctifying growth.

But first, two matters of interpretation: I noted that I had changed one word in the *Christian Counselor's New Testament,* from which I just quoted: it is the word "grace." In the *CCNT,* I translated it "help." Because the word grace is so common, I retained it in the title of the book and when I first quoted this verse. The word "grace" has several meanings, including "unmerited favor" (the best known) and "help" (which is not so well known). In passages where the word applies to believers, it usually means "help," as it does here in II Peter 3:18. Peter is saying that we need the help and the knowledge that the Lord Jesus Christ gives to us. He is the Source of both. Indeed, the "and" in the verse is thought by some to be epexegetical,[1] yielding a rendering something like this: "Help, *even* [i.e., namely] the knowledge of [that comes from] our Lord and Savior, Jesus Christ." Whether or not that is the case, it is obvious that the one sort of help that is mentioned is "knowledge."

There is a second change that I have made in that sentence: I translate the Greek word *en* as "by" instead of "in." I hardly makes sense to speak of growing *in* grace. This becomes clear especially when you recognize that Peter is talking about "help." How would you possibly grow *in* help? In its instrumental use,[2] *en* may be rightly translated "by." The important thing here is this – Jesus gives His people

---

1. This means that the second element (knowledge) further explains the first (help). The kind of help in view is the provision of knowledge that one needs to confront error.

2. To think of this as a spherical dative, inferring that one grows in the sphere of grace, is much more difficult. Either way, Peter speaks of the *help* one receives from Christ, emphasizing how that help involves *knowledge.* Knowledge, of course, is what those who have fallen victim to the twisted teaching of untaught, unstable persons need.

knowledge that enables them to grow strong enough to withstand the false teaching that might otherwise lead them astray. He is relating sanctification, as it produces stability, to knowledge.

The counselor, as a result, must become a teacher of biblical knowledge. True counselors always bring knowledge to the counseling session. That is why a counselor must be a "knowledgeable" person who "rightly handles the Word of truth" (II Timothy 2:15). After all, he is to be concerned about his counselee; that is a given. But he is also to be concerned about those who are unstable and untaught. As Paul taught, "in meekness" he must correct "those who oppose [God's truth], in hope that God may bring them by repentance into the full knowledge of the truth" (II Timothy 2:25). Growth, then, comes through "knowledge." It is questionable whether growth ever occurs apart from it.

Think about that last statement of Peter's for a bit. Peter contrasts untaught instability with certain knowledge. A person simply cannot grow as he should if he is unstable. For example, if someone who has for a time understood the biblical teaching of the perseverance of the saints, subsequently is seduced into questioning that doctrine because of the teaching of someone who does not have a clear knowledge of biblical teaching, it will adversely affect his growth. This flawed teaching may cause him to focus on himself rather than on pleasing God and showing love for others. The sanctification process will be seriously hindered. Indeed, uncertainty of salvation could cause a logjam that might easily set back his spiritual growth significantly.

Paul spoke about the importance of becoming firmly rooted in the Bible so as to become mature in the faith. Here is what he said in Ephesians 4:13 and 14:

> ...until we all attain to the unity of the faith and to the full knowledge of God's Son, to mature manhood, to the point where we become as fully adult as Christ.

> This must happen so that we may no longer be infants, blown about and carried around by every wind of teaching, by human trickery, by craftiness designed to lead to error.

Notice in both passages, the apostles stress the importance of knowledge as the antidote to false teaching.

Now, it is also worthwhile noting that Peter says those who come to deceive will come with the Scriptures. They like to assert the authority of the Scriptures to bolster their errors, but they twist them in order to make them fit their beliefs and teachings. There are too many counselees who will accept as true anything a teacher says so long as he mentions the Scriptures. But here, Peter warns that not everyone who uses the Scriptures may be trusted. Many twist them. So it is not enough for someone to represent himself as a *Bible* teacher. How does he handle the Bible? Is his teaching that of someone who is "untaught" in the Word? There are many who, with very little understanding of what Scripture means, take it upon themselves to teach others. Just because one has the money to buy radio or TV time does not mean he is knowledgeable in the things concerning the faith. Counselees must be taught to examine carefully all new teachings. They should compare them with the historic confessions of the church and ask for their pastor's opinion before accepting them. Because many did not do this, the "untaught" William Miller (who himself was a believer) spawned two Adventist cults![1]

So growth comes by the help that Jesus gives. We have already mentioned that Jesus sent the Holy Spirit to dwell within us to enable us to understand His Word. And one purpose of that understanding is to be able to avoid being deceived by false teaching. John wrote:

> Let that which you have heard from the beginning remain in you... I wrote these things to you about

---

1. The Adventists (eventually becoming the Seventh Day Adventists) and, through them, the Jehovah's Witnesses.

those who are misleading you. But the Anointing that you have received from Him [the Holy Spirit] remains in you and you don't need anybody to teach you. Rather, since His Anointing teaches you about everything (and is true, and doesn't lie), remain in Him even as He has taught you (I John 2:24, 26, 27).

Clearly, one function of the Spirit with whom we were anointed at baptism (cf. I Corinthians 12:13) is to enable us to comprehend and apply what the apostles taught. God's concern is for us to obtain knowledge of Him and His will because knowledge is so closely associated with growth. That knowledge is not extra-biblical but biblical. So then, growth comes from the Spirit, enabling us to become knowledgeable about biblical teaching by helping us to interpret and apply His Word correctly. That is the bottom line.

Every counselor, then, ought to warn about the unstable teachings of untaught persons – who abound in our society. And they must teach counselees the basic truths from Scripture that apply to their situations. Moreover, they would do well to urge every counselee to take a course in Bible interpretation. After all, to send a counselee who has been "led astray" back where people may lead him astray again, unprepared, without warning and buttressing him against such errors as much as possible, is simply poor counseling.

The trouble is that there are too many counselors who are afraid to tackle doctrine – even when it is a large part of a counselee's problem.[1] Not only is that poor counseling, it is usually cowardly. Or, in other cases, the counselor may not know enough doctrine himself to handle the aberrant teachings that his counselee has imbibed. If either of these

---

1. The writers of the New Testament, and Jesus Himself, are not hesitant to refute false doctrine. It is a mistake to think that such refutation can be avoided. While one must refute in meekness, as we have seen, nevertheless, he must do it! The Bible has much to say about this matter.

is true of you, shame on you, counselor! Don't wait another day before hitting the books to discover what you need to know to help that counselee. And study the Scriptures so regularly that the next time there is such a problem, you will be prepared to meet it.[1]

So knowledge brings about growth. It "helps" in many ways. And the help and knowledge that Jesus gives your counselees to assist them to grow in sanctification may very likely be by means of *you*!

---

1. Too many counselors study books about counseling (like this one) rather than the Bible and those books that will help them properly interpret it without twisting it. Unfortunately, it is in books about counseling that one often finds some of the poorest interpretations of the Scriptures!

## Chapter Thirteen
## How Much Growth Is Possible?

In contrast to the perfectionists and the victorious life people, there have been those throughout the history of the church who have taught that very little Christian growth is possible. Their over-emphasis on sin in the regenerate almost cancels out the presence and power of the Holy Spirit, Who is at work in a regenerate person's life sanctifying him. Both of these extreme emphases are unscriptural.

Surely the Spirit, with His sovereign power, is capable of overcoming any sin He wishes. And since He took up residence in Christians to do that work, there should be every expectation that He will be doing it (cf. Philippians 1:6). Surely, as Paul said, God produces in us "both the willingness and the ability to do the things that please Him" (Philippians 2:13). Surely His power enables believers to put behind them many sinful lifestyles (see I Corinthians 6:9–11). Keeping these facts in mind, then, let us explore something of the possibilities for achieving sanctifying growth in counselees.

It is important for the counselor to be clear about the possibilities for achieving growth. Low expectations or ultra-high ones will have a lot to do with how he counsels. Interestingly enough, both of these extremes end up causing the same result: the counselor makes too little effort to bring about change. On the one hand, if little can be expected, the counselor will aim too low and settle for less than he ought. On the other hand, if the counselor thinks that in some instantaneous manner his counselee will be wafted up to heights of victory, obviously there will be little for him to do. Both views tend to limit the amount of counseling activity.

The biblical counselor, however, recognizes that true growth in living for Christ may require much counseling. The counselor and the believer, in cooperation with the Spirit and prayerfully using the Word, must struggle for growth and fight against all the internal and external forces that would inhibit it.

The very image of growth indicates that sanctification takes time, takes cultivation, and takes care. Healthy plants that produce "much fruit" also require pruning by the Word (cf. John 15:1–5[1]). The phrase "much fruit" is important to the discussion that we have undertaken in this chapter. The Lord Jesus not only postulates its possibility but *expects* the believer to produce "much fruit"; when he does not, counseling may be called for. Jesus holds out the prospect of *much* fruit – not very little but also not a hundred percent yield.

In His comments on fruit-bearing, the Lord also told us what it would take for successful fruit-growing. He told the disciples that He had "pruned" them by His "word" (John 15:3). There can be little doubt that the same is true today as well. Once again we see that it is the Word of God – today found only in the Scriptures of the Old and the New Testaments – that brings about sanctification. Therefore, counselors must become aware of the utter importance of the Word for sanctification in counseling.

Of course, the prerequisite to all fruit-bearing is remaining in Christ, Who declared: "Just as the branch can't bear fruit on its own (unless it stays on the vine), so you can't unless you stay in Me" (John 15:4). *Staying* or *remaining* (in the KJV, "abiding") in the vine has to do not with some quietistic "resting" but, rather, with perseverance: "unless a person stays in Me, he is thrown outside like a branch and withers; they gather them, throw them into the fire and burn them" (John 15:6). Clearly, it is not true believers who are discarded and burned, but those who make a false profession of faith. How can they be known? They do not persevere.

---

1. In many ways, the counselor may view himself as a vinedresser whose task is to prune the "plants" that God sends his way so that they may bear much fruit. To do this, he must know how to deftly wield the sharp knife of Scripture in a responsible manner.

But to those who remain until the end, Jesus gives assurance that they will bear much fruit. Not only does He assure us that this is true, He also indicates that it is normal to anticipate this sort of abundance. I cannot stress strongly enough, then, that the believer should settle for nothing less than that which the Lord holds forth – "much fruit."

Again, the manner of growing is to "cleanse" oneself from both inner and outer corruption, as Paul wrote in II Corinthians 7:1, "Since we have these promises, dear friends, we must cleanse ourselves from every pollution of flesh and spirit, completing our holiness out of fear for God." To cleanse from pollution is but another term for pruning (literally, "cleansing") sinful practices. But once more note the "promises" of the Scriptures (quoted in II Corinthians 6:16–18) are the basis for the cleansing process. In the passage quoted from the Old Testament, God commands them to "come out from their midst and *be separate.*" The call to "be separate" is a call to sanctification. Stressing biblical calls to sanctification are of importance in helping counselees to grow. The biblical call must be echoed by the counselor, heard by the counselee, enforced by the Spirit, and performed by His help. When that happens, blossoms will appear, grow, bud, and produce much fruit.

The end of the matter is this: "My Father is glorified by this – that you bear much fruit; then you will be My disciples" (John 15:8). In other words, to be a true disciple is to bear much fruit. If a person does not produce fruit, then we must question his salvation. After all, the goal of the Christian's life ought to be to glorify God. If in some sense he does not bring glory to God, he is not fulfilling his purpose as a disciple. Jesus says fruit in the Christian's life is what spreads God's fame among others. This point agrees with His words in Matthew 7:20: "So it is from their fruit that you will know them." Indeed, all of this is but a further exposition of Jesus' command, "Let your light shine in the presence of people so that they may see your fine deeds and glorify your Father Who is in the heavens" (Matthew 5:16).

There is no question about how much growth is possible – much! That is Christ's word.

## Chapter Fourteen
# Does Suffering Sanctify?

It depends. The Bible certainly gives every indication that God uses trials and suffering to help His children grow – but only when they handle it correctly. At the beginning of his letter, James urges his readers, "My brothers, consider it a happy situation when you fall into trials of various sorts" (James 1:2). How can he say that? He goes on, "knowing that the testing of your faith works endurance" (v. 3). So James explains, testings of all sorts can help a Christian learn how to endure. But then he continues, "Let endurance have its full effect, that you may be complete and entire, lacking nothing" (v. 4). There seems to be in these words a warning that one may curtail the sanctifying process in such a way that its full effect may not be enjoyed. The completion of the process may be cut short. Sanctification through suffering doesn't take place automatically.

This is what so often happens when Christians are in a privileged position to grow: in one way or another, they step in and stop their own growth. What usually happens, as James goes on to say, is that we fail to ask for the "wisdom" that we ought to derive from the experience (v. 5). And when we do ask, we often ask with weak faith, full of doubts about how the trial we are undergoing could possibly be for our sanctification (v. 6).

In such cases, we will receive nothing from the Lord by way of understanding (v. 7) because "a double-minded person is unstable in all his ways" (v. 8). God graciously answers the prayer of faith without reproaching us for our lack of wisdom and grants the wisdom when it is needed to undergo the trial and to grow in grace. It is plain, then, that trials may be a blessing, not in and of themselves (the Christian is not a masochist), but in the results they may produce. Trials can be an integral part of our sanctification.

"But if there were no trials, there would be no need for

endurance." I can hear this objection. Yes, this is true, but we live in a world of sin, and sin brings about "trials of various sorts." The smaller ones teach us how to endure so that when the larger ones appear we know what to do. We will have learned how to endure. In other words, the trials that come may be turned into valuable resources for growth in handling future trials. But to doubt their efficacy is to cut off the benefits. Instead, what we ought to do is ask for wisdom to see how we can profit from each trial.

Here, counselors can be of great benefit in helping counselees to get the most blessing from the various trials they must go through. Very few counselees understand what James said. They must be instructed and helped to see that trials, when handled God's way, are a means of grace – a way in which God makes us more like Christ. Jesus also endured trials and was the better for them.[1] So can we become better through suffering. He learned obedience by means of suffering and achieved salvation for us! Note that more than one benefit may be derived from trials and suffering. Both He and we benefited from His suffering. If even Jesus, as man, had to learn from suffering, then surely we must as well.

Through the ages the people of God have learned how to grow by means of the grace (help) of suffering (i.e., that suffering provides). Listen to these words from Psalm 119:

> Before I was afflicted I went astray, but now I have kept Your Word (v. 67, NKJV).

> It is good that I was afflicted that I might learn Your statutes (v. 71, NKJV).

> Yahweh, I know that Your judgments are righteous, and that it is in faithfulness that You have afflicted me (v. 75).

---

1. "Even though He was a Son, He learned obedience from what he suffered; and having been perfected, He became the Origin of eternal salvation to those who obey Him" (Hebrews 5:8, 9).

Unless Your law had been my delight, long ago I would have perished in my affliction (v. 92).

Affliction and pressure have seized me, but Your commandments are my delight (v. 143).

In all of these verses we see one thing: the Word of God helped the Psalmist to turn affliction into profit. The counselor will be remiss if he does not encourage his counselee when suffering to find the direction, the sustenance he needs, the answers, and the encouragement to handle trials that are found in the Bible.

In Psalm 119:92, it is clear from his words that the psalmist could not have endured the suffering he was experiencing apart from the Scriptures in which he delighted. That "delight," presumably, came from familiarity with the law of God before the suffering so that when it appeared he was able to turn to those truths to sustain him. Otherwise, he might have succumbed to the trial.

Not everyone must know the Bible thoroughly before undergoing trial, however. At an earlier point in his life, the psalmist learned how beneficial the Scriptures are *by undergoing suffering* (v. 71). In verse 67, he makes the point that before his affliction, he wandered out of God's pathways, but his affliction brought him back to the Scriptures to find his way. The trial itself drove him to God's Word so that he might once more learn to walk in His ways.

How was it that the Bible (God's "judgments") instructed and comforted him in trial? He says in verse 75 that from them he learned that all affliction that God sent his way was for his good: "In faithfulness You have afflicted me." God was not bringing something unjust into his life; from His perspective (regardless of what other people meant to do to him[1]) the intention was a faithful one. God had not forsaken him. Actually, He was working out something good for him.

---

1. See also Genesis 50:20. Joseph's brothers planned to do evil to him, but God planned to do good through their evil act and to save the

Paul also noted how his suffering was given for his sanctification, in order to keep him from becoming proud. He had been caught up into the third heaven, had seen wonderful things and was given a "thorn in the flesh" to keep him from boasting (II Corinthians 12:2). This physical affliction (a seriously impairing eye condition, perhaps) helped keep him humble. So even extreme difficulties may be intended by God for a blessing. After praying three times that God would remove the condition, at last he came to see that it was designed by God as a blessing, and he could write about it that way. That passage is one that many counselees have found to be of comfort when they were suffering from some physical illness or affliction. Countering pride may not always be the benefit derived, but some benefit may always be found in sickness if one is on the alert to find it.

So we see that everything depends upon how a trial or affliction is handled. And the way in which one comes to correctly evaluate the trial is by applying the teachings of the Bible to the situation. But the wicked – and even God's people at times – fail to do so. Rather, they may turn farther away from God, or against Him, as the result of trials. Take the case of Pharaoh. Here was a man who had several opportunities to repent and humble himself before God. But instead he hardened his heart!

Look at God's people. Jeremiah wrote,

> O Lord, do not Thy eyes search for truth? Thou hast beaten them, but they felt no rebuke; Thou hast disciplined them, but they spurned correction. They have

---

people of Israel, from whom the Messiah would come, from perishing during the famine. Once again, the double intention – man's and God's – is made clear. Counselors must help counselees to turn from what men intend (which is where their focus so often lies) to what the Bible says God, in faithfulness, is doing for them. Even when they cannot see the outcome until much later, as in Joseph's case, they can be taught the truth of Romans 8:28, 29.

made their faces harder than flint; they have refused to repent (Jeremiah 5:3, Berkeley).

That is exactly the wrong response to suffering. Here were people who named the Name of the Lord *wasting* their suffering. That is the best you can say for them. They failed to profit from it. God sent affliction to bring them to repentance and, instead of repenting, they became hardened. Some counselees will be exactly like that. No matter how you show them God's will from the Scriptures, no matter how severely God punishes them for their sin, their response is the opposite of what it should be. The passage in Jeremiah would be a good one to read to such persons as a warning, hoping that they would stop wasting their suffering.

Contrast the Apostle Paul who spoke often of his sufferings for Christ. Here was a man mightily used of God – partly because he seemed always to benefit from suffering. Listen to these words:

> We are afflicted in all sorts of ways, but not crushed; perplexed, but not given to despair; persecuted, but not deserted; struck down, but not destroyed.... Now all of this is for your sake so that as grace spreads to more and more people it may result in an overflowing of thanksgiving to God's glory (II Corinthians 4:8–9, 15).

It is clear that Paul looked away from the present suffering to the *result* coming from it. In one way or another he saw that his suffering would bless people and glorify God. How important it is for counselees to be taught to do the same! Paul continues,

> As a result, we don't give up, even though our outer person is decaying, because our inner person is being renewed daily. This temporary light affliction is producing for us an eternal weight of glory that is beyond all comparison, since we aren't looking for the things that are seen, but rather for the things that

> are unseen. The things that are seen are temporary,
> but the things that are unseen are eternal (II Corin-
> thians 4:16–18)

It is utterly amazing that Paul could call his suffering "light affliction"! All one need do is to read the lists of sufferings in chapters 6:4–10 and 11:22–29 in this very book of II Corinthians to see how extensive they were. I suggest that you do so for counselees to show what it was that he could call "light afflictions." How could he do it?

He explains by citing two facts: first, he was receiving daily inward renewal from God. Certainly, he was sustained by prayer and the reading of the Word. Second, he kept his eye fixed on eternity. He saw the reward as did the suffering saints of old (Hebrews 11:13–16). Jesus encouraged us to do this in Matthew 6:19 through 21, when He urged us to store up treasures in heaven, and He explained, "Where your treasure is, there is where your heart will be too" (v. 21). Here is the ultimate key to enduring and to benefiting from suffering. Sanctification is achieved as one fixes his heart on the things that are eternal. That is what makes him of earthly good now!

Counselor, do you often talk to your counselees about the *results* of affliction? Do you help them to fix their eyes on eternity? Do you urge them not to lose the blessings of suffering? Do you point them to how sufferings may enable them to grow? You should.

## Chapter Fifteen
# Sanctification and Obedience

Obedience is intimately connected to counseling and to sanctification. In giving the great commission, the Lord Jesus commanded,

> Go, therefore, and disciple all nations, baptizing them into the Name of the Father and of the Son and of the Holy Spirit, teaching them to observe all that I have commanded you (Matthew 28:19, 20).

Here is a command to teach disciples to observe all of Christ's commands. The command to disciple those in "all nations" is in educational terms. It included the task of teaching. But the kind of education that is in view is a Hebrew form of education, not ours. This teaching requires not the mere imparting of facts, but the discipling of those who are taught. It is education that brings about change in the lifestyle of the disciple (student).[1] But notice that the education is pictured by Jesus as teaching that leads to the "observance of His commands." What do these words mean?

First of all, note that this command to disciple and teach comes in a certain context. The word "therefore,"[2] which begins this sentence, refers back to verse 18 in which Jesus declared to the eleven disciples: "All authority in heaven and on earth has been given to Me." Here, proleptically,[3] Jesus declares that all the sovereign authority (Greek, *exousia*) of God had been granted to Him as the God-man over everything and everyone in the heavens and on the earth.

---

1. See the earlier discussion of this matter in Chapter Eleven. For the greatest detail, see my book *Teaching to Observe*.

2. Greek, *oun*.

3. That is, speaking of something that is just about to happen as if it already had happened. At Jesus' ascension He would be "crowned with glory and honor" (Hebrews 2:9).

He is making it clear that as they went[1] preaching the gospel they would be received by all the *Gentiles* (perhaps the better translation of *ethne* here,[2] since that was the unique thing about their mission: the gospel was to go into all the world to all the Gentiles rather than to Jews alone). This reception would lead to discipleship as those who believed were baptized into (became a part of) the church that bears the Name of the Trinity.

Once having matriculated into the school of Christ through baptism (the admitting ordinance into the visible church, which here is pictured as a school), His disciples (pupils, students) were to be *taught*. After all, that is what a school is all about. And what they were to be taught was the commandments of Christ. Now, commandments are given not merely for knowledge; they are handed down to be obeyed by those who receive them. To speak of "observing" (Greek, *terein*) commandments is but another way of saying *obeying* them. Thus the life of the believer is pictured as a life of discipling, in which he is learning to obey Christ's commands to him. It is, therefore, a life of sanctification.

In a similar way, Paul speaks of conversion as a change of masters from sin to God: "But thank God that you, who were once slaves of sin, now have obeyed from the heart the pattern of teaching to which you were handed over" (Romans 6:17). And he goes on to explain:

> In the same way that you presented your members as slaves to uncleanness and lawlessness to bring about more lawlessness, now you must present your

---

1. Literally, "as you go"; there is no command to go. It is *assumed* that they would.

2. The word *ethne* may be rightly translated either "nations" or "Gentiles." Both are equally possible. The New Testament period was one in which the church would consist of converted Jews and Gentiles alike. So already in his day John could speak of those "persons" that Christ "bought for God from every tribe and tongue and people and nation" (Revelation 5:9; see also Revelation 7:9; 20:2, 3).

members as slaves of righteousness to bring about sanctification (Romans 6:19).

Notice how "sanctification" is the new goal of God's redeemed servant over against "lawlessness," which was his goal when he was still the slave of sin. Obeying Christ's *law* from the heart is the same as keeping (observing, obeying) His commandments. So it is quite clear that discipleship, which at its heart consists of learning to obey Christ, is the means of reaching the goal of such teaching – sanctification.[1] There can be no question about the centrality of obedience in discipleship or about its result – sanctification. Calvin understood this centrality and featured it when he wrote, "nothing is more acceptable to him [God] than obedience."[2]

Obedience is always to commands. It is not abstract. There are those who think that there are no commands to be obeyed today but the command to love. That is quite wrong. Not only does Jesus speak of "all things" (everything) that He commanded during His earthly ministry, but also in the books of the New Testament the obvious fact is that Jesus had laid down orders about many things.[3] To

---

1. See also Romans 6:22, where Paul speaks of the "fruit" (*result*) of the new obedience as "sanctification." Thus one "presents" the members of his body to God for the purpose of working righteousness, which comes by obeying the commandments of Christ ("pattern of teaching") from the heart. And the "fruit" of obedience is sanctification. This sanctification, he says, results in "eternal life."

2. *The Institutes of the Christian Religion,* Book 2, Chapter 8, Section 5.

3. In I Corinthians 7:25, Paul writes, "Now I don't have any order from the Lord about virgins," implying that He did give orders about other things. And, through the Spirit, He was now giving orders through the Apostle (v. 40). See also Titus 2:15: "Speak these things; urge and convict, with recognition that you have full authority to give orders. Let nobody disregard you." Clearly, not only in Person, but through the apostles, Jesus Christ gave His people many commands that were to be obeyed. These were given in order to lead to sanctification, as we see. This means that the counselor will set biblical commands before his counselees and expect them to obey them.

obey specific commands, in fact, is the *way in which* one demonstrates his love. Quietism, of the sort that often opposes counseling which points to the specific commands of the Bible, leaves the counselee up a tree. He simply doesn't know what he must do in order to "love." Love becomes an amorphous thing, perhaps in many cases a mere feeling.

But love in the Scriptures is closely associated with action. It is not passive. "God so loved the world that He *gave...*" (John 3:16; cf. Gal 2:20; Ephesians 5:25). And it is associated with commandments, such as "love your enemies" (Matthew 5:44) which was one of the commandments that Christ gave us to obey. Note that love is *commanded*. It takes place when one *obeys* (clearly, it is more than a feeling). But how is it to be fulfilled? To *show* love to one's enemies, he is to *give* him something to eat or drink if he is hungry or thirsty (Romans 12:20).[1] In John 14:15, Jesus sums all of this up in one pregnant explanation: "If you love Me, keep My commandments." Nothing more on the point need be said!

"But that sounds like legalism," someone may say. One of the most frequently expressed errors is to label the call to obedience to Christ's commands "legalistic." Every counselor will face this false charge from time to time. Actually, there is much talk about legalism, but very little explanation of it. The term is loosely slung about without precise understanding. One reason for this is that legalism has been often referred to but very seldom discussed at length. There are few discussions of the matter in print (when found, they are usually but a part of some other discussion, as in this chapter). I once searched through two voluminous seminary libraries for books on the subject and found none in one and only one in the other. And in the scattered, brief references to legalism that one does find, legalism is

---

1. The principle is to do what you are able to do to meet an enemy's need.

almost always discussed in its relationship to justification not to sanctification.

In terms of legalism's relationship to justification, legalism reeks of a view of salvation by merit.[1] The problem that Paul fought was in relationship to the judaizing of the churches. He was interested not only in the matter of the false teaching of salvation (justification) by works, but also in teaching of sanctification (growing) by works alone. He wrote, for instance:

> Galatians, you are stupid! Who has put a spell on you, you before whose eyes Jesus Christ Jesus Christ was placarded as the crucified One? Tell me this one thing: did you receive the Spirit from works of law, or from hearing with faith? Are you really so stupid? Having begun by the Spirit are you now going to be completed by the flesh? (Galatians 3:1–3)

His concern was to show that the process of sanctification, or being "completed" (Greek, *epiteleo*) by works, was not what Christian living is all about. Later on, in Galatians 5, Paul shows that the characteristics of sanctification (or holiness) that he lists are truly the fruit of the *Spirit*. Legalism, then, is a matter of seeking to become sanctified by works *apart from the Spirit*. However, it is not wrong to insist on obedience *by means of the Spirit*. In terms of counseling, legalism is not a matter of insisting on obedience to Christ's commands, but of teaching that *mere conformity to* those commands will enable counselees to grow in holiness. It consists of depending on those commandments to change the counselee rather than depending on the Spirit to enable him to change.

So there is a legalism of thought and attitude as well as a legalism of action. The first precedes the second. If an act

---

1. In relationship to justification, counselors must be careful not to counsel unbelievers. To do so is to cause them to think that they please God by moving from one unbiblical lifestyle to another. I have discussed this matter earlier in the book.

itself is considered meritorious, the counselee will not only take unfounded pride in what he does (rather than giving the credit to God); but in the end will also fail to observe Christ's commandments. That is because he will not have obeyed "from the heart." To obey from the heart is to obey genuinely; it means that outward conformity alone is unacceptable. Jesus again and again spoke of the inner intent as necessary to the acceptability of the outer action (cf. Matthew 5:27–28). The inner intent of the counselee must correspond to the inner intent of the command. The rich young ruler (Luke 18:18–23) obeyed God's commands outwardly, but loved money more than God or his neighbor. Christ's assignment to sell all he had and give the money he received to the poor and then to follow Him exposed his interior thinking and attitude that was out of sync with his outer conformity. He obeyed, but not "from the heart."

To obey in human wisdom and strength, then, is legalism. But to obey the Word by the Spirit is not. All other forms of counseling are legalistic; biblical counseling alone assumes that the Spirit is necessary in effecting sanctification. He is the "Spirit of holiness" (Romans 1:4) Who works through His Word (John 17:17) to change both actions and intentions. When counselors help counselees to develop new biblical habits to replace old ones, for instance, they encourage them to ask God to change not only externals but also to change their hearts. Peter speaks of "hearts trained in greed" (II Peter 2:14). The heart is where the habit is. "Heart," in Scripture, includes the brain and the mind. The heart must be changed as the habit is; the habit will be changed as the heart is. The one cannot be divorced from the other. Holiness is first and foremost an inside job! To encourage counselees merely to change their outer behavior is to create hypocritical counselees and to make God out to be nothing more than a *decorative* God Who superficially paints over the rotten wood beneath! The biblical counselor must stress prayer, the work of the Spirit, and the Word in enabling him to obey. God is an Interior Decorator.

Legalism, in connection with counseling, is setting a counselee out on a pathway that is doomed to failure because it sets him out to do what he cannot do alone. He must be aided by the knowledge that comes from the Word and the insight and power that comes from the Spirit. Counselors will take heed to this matter because it is central to pleasing God by properly breaking the logjam that impedes sanctification.

But how does one obey that which he does not want to obey? If he does, isn't that legalism? I have heard people say such things. On the one hand, if he obeys *merely* out of duty, of course, that is wrong. But, on the other hand, he may rightly obey when he loathes doing so. "Really?" you ask. Yes. Think of Christ, Who did not want to go to the cross, Who sweat drops of blood over contemplating becoming viewed as a sinner by His Father. He did so, but not because He wanted to. Similarly, a counselee may be called on to do what he does not want to do (for example, loving an enemy). He may ask, "But how can that be? Isn't that the height of legalism? Pharisaism?"

Not if what he does is done out of love for God! One must have the inner desire to please God when out of duty he obeys a commandment that is not pleasant to obey. A housewife cleans the toilets not because she enjoys the chore but because she loves her family. A counselee may be called on to obey a command out of love for God and his neighbor, even when he does not look forward to the task itself. That is what must be stressed. The counselee must understand that in his inner person, he must not do anything God commands for brownie points; he must obey out of love.

The importance of obedience in its relationship to sanctification through the Spirit is plainly stated by Peter in I Peter 1:2 where Peter says that the Spirit sanctifies so that we may obey. One grows by obedience, but that obedience – properly accomplished through the wisdom and power of the Spirit – is itself the result of previous sanctification.

When the Spirit sanctifies in order to enable us to obey, He so changes our desires and abilities that we are able to do those tasks which are undesirable in themselves (cf. Philippians 2:13). So intimately connected are sanctification and obedience then that, once begun, they each produce the other in a chicken-and-egg fashion. The counselor who recognizes this dynamic may break in at either the point of obedience or at the point of thought and intent, so long as he ties both of these together as the Bible does.

## Chapter Sixteen
# Conclusion

One thing ought to be unmistakable: sanctification is critical to counseling. Indeed, as we have seen, counseling is also critical to sanctification. The two stand or fall together. If you are speaking of truly Christian counseling, you are speaking about counseling that assists the process of sanctification whenever it becomes slowed down, halted, or reversed. In fact, the purpose of biblical counseling is nothing other than to enable the Christian to become more like Christ.

On the other hand, a measure of sanctification in the counselee is required for counseling to succeed. The counselee must repent of sin (itself a step in sanctification) in order to break many logjams. He must then take other sanctification steps in order to move ahead with fruit that will not only give evidence of, but also shore up, repentance. So once begun, the process reinforces itself. That shows how intimately the two are bound up in one another.

There is no doubt that, in order to counsel biblically, a counselor must understand sanctification as it is set forth in the Scriptures. If a would-be counselor has a faulty view of sanctification, he will counsel wrongly. That is why this book is necessary. It is intended both to warn and to instruct. As one who would counsel, if you don't fully understand sanctification, if you have any doubts about any aspect of it, if you are unsure that counseling is deeply involved in the sanctification process, please do not counsel until you have settled all these matters biblically. I cannot say it strongly enough – simply stop, study, and learn!

I have shown that counseling is not important in itself, and if logjams in the process of sanctification did not occur, it would be unnecessary. But they do occur, so counseling is necessary. Proper counseling is dependent on a proper doctrinal understanding of sanctification, once more proving that counseling is doctrinal. Bill Goode, former director of the National Association of Nouthetic Counselors, was absolutely correct when he stated that "all counseling problems are theological problems." I would add that all counseling solutions are theological solutions!